Contents

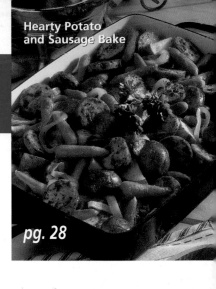

Hearty Potato
and Sausage Bake

pg. 28

Cheesy Deluxe
Primavera Mac Skillet

pg. 104

D0101032

Steak and
Black Bean Chili

pg. 168

Velveeta® Spicy Chicken Spaghetti

12 ounces spaghetti, uncooked
4 boneless skinless chicken breast halves (about 1¼ pounds), cut into strips
1 pound (16 ounces) VELVEETA® Pasteurized Prepared Cheese Product, cut up
1 can (10¾ ounces) condensed cream of chicken soup
1 can (10 ounces) diced tomatoes and green chilies, undrained
1 can (4½ ounces) sliced mushrooms, drained
⅓ cup milk

1. Cook pasta as directed on package; drain. Return to same pan.

2. Spray skillet with no stick cooking spray. Add chicken; cook and stir on medium-high heat 4 to 5 minutes or until cooked through. Add Velveeta, soup, tomatoes and green chilies, mushrooms and milk; stir on low heat until Velveeta is melted. Add chicken mixture to pasta; toss to coat. Spoon into greased 13×9-inch baking dish.

3. Bake at 350°F for 35 to 40 minutes or until hot.   *Makes 6 to 8 servings*

Prep Time: 5 minutes
Bake Time: 40 minutes

A hearty meal all in

one casserole dish

means less time

preparing and

cleaning up. So get

out of the kitchen

and let your oven do

the work for you.

Velveeta® Spicy Chicken Spaghetti

Chicken Enchiladas

1 whole chicken (about 3 pounds), cut into 8 pieces
3 fresh poblano chilies, roasted, peeled, seeded, deveined and diced
1 large tomato, peeled, seeded and chopped
½ cup finely chopped white onion
1 clove garlic, minced
½ teaspoon ground cumin
¼ teaspoon salt
½ cup chicken broth
1½ cups heavy cream
12 corn tortillas (6-inch diameter)
2 cups (8 ounces) shredded queso Chihuahua or Monterey Jack cheese
Green onions and slivered red bell peppers for garnish

1. Place chicken in single layer in 12-inch skillet. Sprinkle with chilies, tomato, white onion, garlic, cumin and salt; add broth. Bring to a boil over medium-high heat. Reduce heat. Cover; simmer 1 hour or until chicken is tender.

2. Remove chicken from skillet with tongs, shaking off vegetable pieces. Let stand until cool enough to handle.

3. Skim and discard fat from skillet. Bring remaining broth mixture to a boil over medium-high heat. Boil 4 to 8 minutes until mixture is reduced to 2 cups. Pour reduced broth mixture into 13×9-inch baking dish.

4. Remove and discard skin and bones from chicken. Using fingers, pull chicken into coarse shreds.

5. Preheat oven to 375°F. Heat cream in medium skillet over medium heat to just below boiling; remove from heat.

6. Dip 1 tortilla in cream with tongs a few seconds or until limp. Remove, draining off excess cream. Spread about 3 tablespoons chicken down center of tortilla.

7. Roll up; place on sauce in baking dish. Repeat with remaining tortillas, cream and chicken. Pour any remaining cream over enchiladas.

8. Sprinkle cheese over enchiladas. Bake 25 to 30 minutes until sauce is bubbly and cheese is melted. Garnish, if desired. *Makes 4 to 6 servings*

Chicken Enchiladas

4

Chicken Caesar Tetrazzini

8 ounces uncooked spaghetti
2 cups shredded or cubed cooked chicken
1 cup chicken broth
1 cup HIDDEN VALLEY® Caesar Dressing
1 jar (4½ ounces) sliced mushrooms, drained
½ cup grated Parmesan cheese
2 tablespoons dry bread crumbs

Cook spaghetti according to package directions. Drain and combine with chicken, broth, dressing and mushrooms in a large mixing bowl. Place mixture in a 2-quart casserole. Mix together cheese and bread crumbs; sprinkle over spaghetti mixture. Bake at 350°F. for 25 minutes or until casserole is hot and bubbly.

Makes 4 servings

Turkey Broccoli Bake

1 bag (16 ounces) frozen broccoli cuts, thawed, drained
2 cups cubed cooked turkey or chicken
2 cups soft bread cubes
8 ounces sliced American cheese, divided
1 jar (12 ounces) HEINZ® HomeStyle Turkey or Chicken Gravy
½ cup undiluted evaporated milk
    Dash pepper

In buttered 9-inch square baking dish, layer broccoli, turkey, bread cubes and cheese. Combine gravy, milk and pepper; pour over cheese. Bake in 375°F oven, 40 minutes. Let stand 5 minutes before serving.

Makes 6 servings

Chicken Caesar Tetrazzini

Fast 'n' Fancy Casserole

1 package (10 ounces) PERDUE® SHORT CUTS® Fresh Original Roasted Carved Chicken
    Breast
1 package (8 to 10 ounces) frozen peas and carrots
1 jar (17 ounces) Alfredo sauce
6 ounces (1½ cups uncooked) fusilli, rotelle or ziti, cooked and drained
1 package (8 ounces) shredded Italian cheeses with seasonings (2 cups), divided
    Salt and ground pepper to taste

Preheat oven to 375°F. Grease 8- to 9-inch square baking dish. In medium bowl, combine chicken, vegetables, sauce, pasta and 1 cup cheese. Season with salt and pepper; mix well. Top with remaining cheese. Bake 20 minutes or until bubbly. *Makes 4 servings*

Prep Time: 5 to 10 minutes
Cook Time: 20 minutes

8

Herbed Chicken and Potatoes

2 medium all-purpose potatoes, thinly sliced (about 1 pound)
4 bone-in chicken breast halves (about 2 pounds)*
1 envelope LIPTON® RECIPE SECRETS® Savory Herb with Garlic Soup Mix
⅓ cup water
1 tablespoon olive or vegetable oil

*Substitution: Use 1 (2½- to 3-pound) chicken; cut into serving pieces.

1. Preheat oven to 425°F. In 13×9-inch baking or roasting pan, add potatoes; arrange chicken over potatoes.

2. Pour soup mix blended with water and oil over chicken and potatoes.

3. Bake uncovered 40 minutes or until chicken is no longer pink in center and potatoes are tender. *Makes 4 servings*

Ravioli with Homemade Tomato Sauce

　3 cloves garlic, peeled
½ cup fresh basil leaves
　3 cups seeded, peeled tomatoes, cut into quarters
　2 tablespoons tomato paste
　2 tablespoons fat-free Italian salad dressing
　1 tablespoon balsamic vinegar
¼ teaspoon black pepper
　1 package (9 ounces) refrigerated reduced-fat cheese ravioli
　2 cups shredded spinach leaves
　1 cup (4 ounces) shredded part-skim mozzarella cheese

MICROWAVE DIRECTIONS

1. To prepare tomato sauce, process garlic in food processor until coarsely chopped. Add basil; process until coarsely chopped. Add tomatoes, tomato paste, salad dressing, vinegar and pepper; process using on/off pulsing action until tomatoes are chopped.

2. Spray 9-inch square microwavable dish with nonstick cooking spray. Spread 1 cup tomato sauce in dish. Layer half of ravioli and spinach over tomato sauce. Repeat layers with 1 cup tomato sauce and remaining ravioli and spinach. Top with remaining 1 cup tomato sauce.

3. Cover with plastic wrap; refrigerate 1 to 8 hours. Vent plastic wrap. Microwave at MEDIUM (50% power) 20 minutes or until pasta is tender and hot. Sprinkle with cheese. Microwave at HIGH 3 minutes or just until cheese melts. Let stand, covered, 5 minutes before serving.

Makes 6 servings

9

Mexican Lasagna

4 boneless skinless chicken breast halves
2 tablespoons vegetable oil
2 teaspoons chili powder
1 teaspoon ground cumin
1 can (14½ ounces) diced tomatoes with garlic, drained
1 can (8 ounces) tomato sauce
1 teaspoon hot pepper sauce (optional)
1 cup part-skim ricotta cheese
1 can (4 ounces) diced green chilies
¼ cup chopped fresh cilantro, divided
12 (6-inch) corn tortillas
1 cup (4 ounces) shredded Cheddar cheese

Preheat oven to 375°F. Cut chicken into ½-inch pieces.

Heat oil in large skillet over medium heat. Add chicken, chili powder and cumin. Cook
4 minutes or until chicken is tender, stirring occasionally. Stir in diced tomatoes, tomato sauce
and hot pepper sauce, if desired; bring to a boil. Reduce heat; simmer 2 minutes.

Combine ricotta cheese, chilies and 2 tablespoons cilantro in small bowl; mix until well
blended.

Spoon half of chicken mixture into 12×8-inch baking dish. Top with 6 tortillas, ricotta cheese
mixture, remaining 6 tortillas, remaining chicken mixture, Cheddar cheese and remaining
2 tablespoons cilantro. Bake 25 minutes or until heated through.   *Makes 6 to 8 servings*

*Choose mild green chilies for this recipe. If diced tomatoes with garlic are not
available, you may add one clove minced garlic to a can of diced tomatoes.*

Mexican Lasagna

Zesty Turkey Pot Pie

1 tablespoon vegetable oil
1 small onion, finely chopped
1 jalapeño pepper,* seeded and minced
1 pound ground turkey
1 package (16 ounces) frozen mixed vegetables
½ teaspoon dried thyme leaves
½ teaspoon black pepper
2 cans (10¾ ounces each) golden mushroom soup
1 package (11 ounces) refrigerated breadsticks (12 breadsticks)

*Jalapeño peppers can sting and irritate the skin; wear rubber gloves when handling peppers and do not touch eyes. Wash hands after handling peppers.

1. Preheat oven to 350°F.

2. Heat oil in large skillet over medium heat. Add onion and jalapeño pepper; cook and stir 5 minutes or until tender. Add turkey; cook and stir until no longer pink, stirring to separate meat. Stir in vegetables, thyme and pepper. Cook 5 minutes until vegetables are thawed. Stir in soup. Cook 5 minutes or until heated through.

3. Spoon turkey mixture into greased 13×9-inch casserole. Pull and stretch breadsticks to lengthen, pressing ends together if necessary to reach across baking dish. Arrange breadsticks in lattice pattern over turkey, trimming ends. Bake 15 to 20 minutes or until breadsticks are golden.   *Makes 6 servings*

Note: Mixture must be hot when spooned into casserole or breadsticks will become gummy on the bottom.

Zesty Turkey Pot Pie

Chicken Normandy Style

2 tablespoons butter, divided
3 cups peeled, thinly sliced apples (about 3 apples)
1 pound ground chicken
¼ cup apple brandy or apple juice
1 can (10¾ ounces) cream of chicken soup
¼ cup finely chopped green onions, green part only
2 teaspoons fresh minced sage *or* ½ teaspoon dried sage leaves
¼ teaspoon pepper
1 package (12 ounces) egg noodles, cooked and drained

1. Preheat oven to 350°F.

2. Melt 1 tablespoon butter in 12-inch nonstick skillet. Add apple slices; cook and stir over medium heat 7 to 10 minutes or until tender. Remove apple slices from skillet.

3. Add ground chicken to same skillet; cook and stir over medium heat until brown, breaking up with spoon. Stir in apple brandy and cook 2 minutes. Stir in soup, green onions, sage, pepper and apple slices. Simmer 5 minutes.

4. Toss noodles with remaining 1 tablespoon butter. Spoon into well-greased 9-inch square pan. Top with chicken mixture. Bake for 15 minutes or until hot.   *Makes 4 servings*

Note: Ground turkey, ground pork or tofu crumbles may be substituted for the ground chicken, if desired.

14

For this recipe choose apples that have a sweet rather than a tart flavor. Fugi and Braeburn apples work well.

Chicken Normandy Style

Tuscan Noodle Bake

½ pound Italian sausage, casings removed and sausage crumbled
½ pound BUTTERBALL® Ground Turkey
1 cup chopped onion
1 teaspoon fresh minced garlic
1 can (15 ounces) HUNT'S® Tomato Sauce
1 can (14.5 ounces) HUNT'S® Whole Tomatoes, undrained and crushed
1 can (6 ounces) sliced mushrooms, drained
1 can (2¼ ounces) sliced black olives, drained
¼ cup chopped fresh parsley
1 teaspoon dried basil leaves
1 teaspoon dried oregano leaves
¼ teaspoon pepper
¼ cup TREASURE CAVE® Shredded Parmesan Cheese
½ package (12 ounces) wide egg noodles, cooked and drained
1 cup shredded mozzarella cheese

16

In large Dutch oven, brown sausage and turkey with onion and garlic until meat is no longer pink; drain. Add remaining ingredients except Parmesan cheese, noodles and mozzarella cheese; simmer 5 minutes. Stir in Parmesan cheese and noodles; blend well. Pour noodle mixture into greased 13×9×2-inch baking dish. Bake, covered, at 350°F for 20 minutes. Sprinkle mozzarella cheese over noodle mixture and bake, uncovered, for an additional 5 to 7 minutes. *Makes 6 to 8 servings*

Chicken Parmesan Noodle Bake

1 package (12 ounces) extra-wide noodles
4 boneless, skinless chicken breast halves
¼ teaspoon rosemary, crushed
2 cans (14½ ounces each) DEL MONTE® Diced Tomatoes with Basil, Garlic & Oregano
½ cup (2 ounces) shredded mozzarella cheese
¼ cup (1 ounce) grated Parmesan cheese

1. Preheat oven to 450°F.

2. Cook noodles according to package directions; drain.

3. Meanwhile, sprinkle chicken with rosemary; season with salt and pepper, if desired. Arrange chicken in 13×9-inch baking dish. Bake, uncovered, 20 minutes or until chicken is no longer pink in center. Drain; remove chicken from dish.

4. Drain tomatoes, reserving liquid. In large bowl, toss reserved liquid with noodles; place in baking dish. Top with chicken and tomatoes; sprinkle with cheeses.

5. Bake 10 minutes or until heated through. Sprinkle with additional Parmesan cheese and garnish, if desired. *Makes 4 servings*

Prep & Cook Time: 35 minutes

Chicken Tetrazzini

   8 ounces uncooked spaghetti, broken in half
   3 tablespoons butter, divided
   ¼ cup all-purpose flour
   1 teaspoon salt
   ½ teaspoon paprika
   ½ teaspoon celery salt
   ⅛ teaspoon pepper
   2 cups milk
   1 cup chicken broth
   3 cups chopped cooked chicken
   1 can (4 ounces) mushrooms, drained
   ¼ cup pimiento strips
   ¾ cup (3 ounces) grated Wisconsin Parmesan cheese, divided

In large saucepan, cook spaghetti according to package directions; drain. Return to same saucepan; add 1 tablespoon butter. Stir until melted. Set aside. In 3-quart saucepan, melt remaining 2 tablespoons butter over medium heat; stir in flour, salt, paprika, celery salt and pepper. Remove from heat; gradually stir in milk and chicken broth. Cook over medium heat, stirring constantly, until thickened. Add chicken, mushrooms, pimiento, spaghetti and ¼ cup cheese; heat thoroughly. Place chicken mixture on ovenproof platter or in shallow casserole; sprinkle remaining ½ cup cheese over top. Broil about 3 inches from heat until lightly browned. *Makes 6 to 8 servings*

*Favorite recipe from **Wisconsin Milk Marketing Board***

17

Chicken 'n' Rice Filled Cabbage Rolls

12 large whole green cabbage leaves
¾ medium onion, chopped
1 clove garlic, minced
1 tablespoon vegetable oil
1 can (15 ounces) tomato sauce
½ cup water
3 tablespoons packed light brown sugar
3 tablespoons lemon juice
⅛ teaspoon ground allspice
3 cups finely chopped cooked chicken
1 cup cooked rice, cooled
1 egg, beaten
¾ teaspoon salt
⅛ teaspoon black pepper

18

Bring 6 cups water to a boil in Dutch oven over high heat. Add cabbage leaves and reduce heat to low. Simmer, covered, 10 to 12 minutes or until cabbage leaves are tender. Drain; rinse under cold running water.

Cook and stir onion and garlic in oil in large skillet over medium heat 6 to 8 minutes or until tender. Remove ½ cup onion mixture. Add tomato sauce, ½ cup water, brown sugar, lemon juice and allspice to onion mixture in skillet. Cook, uncovered, 10 minutes, stirring occasionally.

Combine reserved onion mixture, chicken, rice, egg, salt and black pepper; mix well. Place about ⅓ cup mixture in center of each cabbage leaf. Fold sides over filling; roll up.

Preheat oven to 350°F. Spread ½ cup tomato sauce over bottom of 13×9-inch baking dish. Arrange cabbage rolls, seam side down, over sauce. Spoon remaining sauce evenly over cabbage rolls; cover with foil. Bake 1 hour and 15 minutes or until very tender.

Makes 4 to 6 servings

Chicken 'n' Rice Filled Cabbage Rolls

Moroccan Chicken, Apricot & Almond Casserole

1 pound ground chicken*
¾ teaspoon salt, divided
¼ teaspoon ground cinnamon
¼ teaspoon black pepper
1 tablespoon olive oil
1 small onion, peeled and chopped
1 cup sliced dried apricots
½ teaspoon red pepper flakes
½ teaspoon ground ginger
1 can (28 ounces) diced tomatoes, undrained
1 can (10¾ ounces) chicken broth
½ cup water
1 cup large-pearl couscous**
¼ cup sliced almonds, toasted

*Ground turkey or lamb may be substituted for the ground chicken, if desired.

**Large-pearl couscous, which is the size of barley, is available in many supermarkets. If it is not available, substitute regular small-grain couscous.

20

1. Preheat oven to 325°F.

2. Combine ground chicken, ½ teaspoon salt, cinnamon and black pepper in medium bowl. Shape into 1-inch balls. Heat oil in large skillet. Add chicken and brown on all sides. Remove to a plate. Add onion and apricots to skillet. Cook mixture 5 minutes over medium heat or until onion is tender. Stir in remaining ¼ teaspoon salt, red pepper flakes, ginger and tomatoes with juice. Simmer 5 minutes.

3. Meanwhile, bring chicken broth and water to a boil in small saucepan. Stir in large-pearl couscous.*** Reduce heat; cover and simmer 10 minutes or until couscous is tender and almost all liquid has is absorbed. Drain if necessary.

4. Spoon couscous into greased 11×7-inch casserole dish. Top with chicken and spoon on tomato mixture. Bake 20 minutes or until chicken is no longer pink in center. Sprinkle with almonds.   *Makes 4 to 6 servings*

***To cook small-grain couscous follow package directions using 1 cup chicken broth in place of water. Remove from heat and let stand 5 minutes or until all liquid is absorbed. Fluff with a fork.

*Moroccan Chicken, Apricot &
Almond Casserole*

Zesty Italian Stuffed Peppers

   3 bell peppers (green, red or yellow), cut in half lengthwise, seeds discarded
   1 pound ground beef
   1 jar (14 ounces) spaghetti sauce
1⅓ cups *French's*® French Fried Onions, divided
   2 tablespoons *Frank's*® *RedHot*® Cayenne Pepper Sauce
   ½ cup uncooked instant rice
   ¼ cup sliced ripe olives
   1 cup (4 ounces) shredded mozzarella cheese

Preheat oven to 400°F. Place peppers, cut side up, in shallow 2-quart baking dish; set aside.

Place beef in large microwavable bowl. Microwave on HIGH 5 minutes or until meat is browned, stirring once. Drain. Stir in spaghetti sauce, ⅔ cup French Fried Onions, **Frank's RedHot** Sauce, rice and olives. Spoon evenly into bell pepper halves.

Cover; bake 35 minutes or until bell peppers are tender. Uncover; sprinkle with cheese and remaining ⅔ cup onions. Bake 1 minute or until onions are golden.   *Makes 6 servings*

Prep Time: 10 minutes
Cook Time: 36 minutes

22

Monterey Black Bean Tortilla Supper

   1 pound ground beef, browned and drained
1½ cups bottled salsa
   1 (15-ounce) can black beans, drained
   4 (8-inch) flour tortillas
   2 cups (8 ounces) shredded Wisconsin Monterey Jack cheese*

*For authentic Mexican flavor, substitute 2 cups shredded Wisconsin Queso Blanco.

Heat oven to 400°F. Combine ground beef, salsa and beans. In lightly greased 2-quart round casserole, layer one tortilla, ⅔ cup meat mixture and ½ cup cheese. Repeat layers three times. Bake 30 minutes or until heated through.   *Makes 5 to 6 servings*

Favorite recipe from **Wisconsin Milk Marketing Board**

Zesty Italian Stuffed Pepper

Spaghetti Bake

1 pound BOB EVANS® Dinner Link Sausage (regular or Italian)
1 (8-ounce) can tomato sauce
1 (6-ounce) can tomato paste
1 (4-ounce) can sliced mushrooms, drained
½ teaspoon salt
½ teaspoon dried basil leaves
½ teaspoon dried oregano leaves
6 ounces spaghetti, cooked according to package directions and drained
⅓ cup shredded mozzarella cheese
2 tablespoons grated Parmesan cheese
Fresh basil leaves and tomato slices (optional)

Preheat oven to 375°F. Cut sausage links into bite-size pieces. Cook in medium skillet over medium heat until browned, stirring occasionally. Drain off any drippings; set aside. Combine tomato sauce, tomato paste, mushrooms, salt, dried basil and oregano in large bowl. Add spaghetti and reserved sausage; mix well. Spoon into lightly greased 1½-quart casserole dish; sprinkle with cheeses. Bake 20 to 30 minutes or until heated through. Garnish with fresh basil and tomato slices, if desired. Serve hot. Refrigerate leftovers. *Makes 4 servings*

24

Italian sausage, which is a good choice for this casserole, owes its distinctive sweet licoricelike flavor to fennel seeds or anise seeds. It is available in both hot and mild varieties.

Spaghetti Bake

Pork Chops and Apple Stuffing Bake

6 (¾-inch-thick) boneless pork loin chops (about 1½ pounds)
¼ teaspoon salt
⅛ teaspoon black pepper
1 tablespoon vegetable oil
1 small onion, chopped
2 ribs celery, chopped
2 Granny Smith apples, peeled, cored and coarsely chopped (about 2 cups)
1 can (14½ ounces) reduced-sodium chicken broth
1 can (10¾ ounces) condensed cream of celery soup, undiluted
¼ cup dry white wine
6 cups herb-seasoned stuffing cubes

Preheat oven to 375°F. Spray 13×9-inch baking dish with nonstick cooking spray.

Season both sides of pork chops with salt and pepper. Heat oil in large deep skillet over medium-high heat until hot. Add chops and cook until browned on both sides, turning once. Remove chops from skillet; set aside.

Add onion and celery to same skillet. Cook and stir 3 minutes or until onion is tender. Add apples; cook and stir 1 minute. Add broth, soup and wine; mix well. Bring to a simmer; remove from heat. Stir in stuffing cubes until evenly moistened.

Spread stuffing mixture evenly in prepared dish. Place pork chops on top of stuffing; pour any accumulated juices over chops.

Cover tightly with foil and bake 30 to 40 minutes or until pork chops are juicy and barely pink in center.   *Makes 6 servings*

Pork Chop and Apple Stuffing Bake

Hearty Potato and Sausage Bake

1 pound new potatoes, cut in halves or quarters
1 large onion, sliced
½ pound baby carrots
2 tablespoons butter, melted
1 teaspoon salt
1 teaspoon garlic powder
½ teaspoon dried thyme leaves
½ teaspoon black pepper
1 pound cooked chicken sausage or turkey sausage

Preheat oven to 400°F. Spray 13×9-inch baking pan with nonstick cooking spray.

Combine potatoes, onion, carrots, butter, salt, garlic powder, thyme and pepper in large bowl. Toss to coat evenly.

Place potato mixture into prepared pan; bake, uncovered, 30 minutes. Add sausage to potato mixture; mix well. Continue to bake 15 to 20 minutes or until potatoes are tender and golden brown.   *Makes 4 to 6 servings*

New potatoes are small young potatoes. They may be any variety, but most often they are round red potatoes. Their sugar content has not been completely converted to starch so they have a crisp, waxy texture.

Hearty Potato and Sausage Bake

Baked Pasta with Beef and Beans

¼ cup CRISCO® Oil,* divided
½ pound uncooked mostaccioli or penne pasta
1 pound ground beef *or* ½ pound ground beef and ½ pound Italian sausage
1 small onion, peeled and chopped
2 teaspoons jarred minced garlic *or* 1 large garlic clove, peeled and minced
1 can (14½ ounces) chopped tomatoes, drained
1 tablespoon tomato paste
1 teaspoon Italian seasoning
½ teaspoon salt
¼ teaspoon freshly ground black pepper
1 can (8 ounces) kidney beans, drained and rinsed
¼ cup freshly grated Parmesan cheese
1 cup (4 ounces) shredded mozzarella or provolone cheese

*Use your favorite Crisco Oil product.

1. Heat oven to 400°F.

2. Bring large pot of salted water to a boil. Add 2 tablespoons oil and pasta. Cook pasta according to package directions until al dente. Drain.

3. While pasta is cooking, heat large skillet on medium-high heat. Add beef. Cook 3 minutes, breaking up with fork, or until no longer pink. Remove from pan. Discard drippings. Wipe out skillet.

4. Heat remaining 2 tablespoons oil in skillet on medium-high heat. Add onion and garlic. Cook 3 minutes, or until onion is translucent. Return beef to pan. Add tomatoes, tomato paste, Italian seasoning, salt and pepper. Stir well. Cook 5 minutes.

5. Combine pasta, meat mixture and beans in 13×9×2-inch baking dish. Sprinkle with cheeses. Bake at 400°F for 20 to 30 minutes, or until cheese is melted. Serve immediately.

Makes 4 servings

Note: The dish can be prepared a day in advance of baking and refrigerated, tightly covered with plastic wrap. If chilled, bake at 375°F for 35 to 45 minutes.

Preparation Time: 30 minutes
Total Time: 50 to 60 minutes

Southwest Ham 'n Cheese Quiche

    4 (8-inch) flour tortillas
    2 tablespoons butter or margarine, melted
    2 cups pizza 4-cheese blend
 1½ cups (8 ounces) diced CURE 81® ham
    ½ cup sour cream
    ¼ cup salsa
    3 eggs, beaten
      Salsa
      Sour cream

Heat oven to 350°F. Cut 3 tortillas in half. Place remaining whole tortilla in bottom of greased 10-inch quiche dish or tart pan; brush with melted butter. Arrange tortilla halves around edge of dish, rounded sides up, overlapping to form pastry shell. Brush with remaining butter. Place 9-inch round cake pan inside quiche dish. Bake 5 minutes. Cool; remove cake pan. In bowl, combine cheese and ham. Stir in ½ cup sour cream, ¼ cup salsa and eggs. Pour into tortilla shell. Bake 55 to 60 minutes or until knife inserted in center comes out clean. Let stand 5 minutes. Serve with additional salsa and sour cream.   *Makes 6 servings*

31

Sausage and Polenta Casserole

    1 tablespoon olive oil
    1 cup chopped mushrooms
    1 small red bell pepper, cored, seeded and diced
    1 small onion, diced
    1 pound hot or mild bulk Italian sausage
    1 jar (28 to 30 ounces) meatless pasta sauce
    1 roll (16 to 18 ounces) polenta

1. Preheat oven to 350°F.

2. Heat oil in large skillet. Add mushrooms, bell pepper and onion; cook and stir over medium heat 5 minutes or until tender. Add sausage; cook and stir until sausage is brown, breaking into small pieces with spoon. Drain. Stir in pasta sauce and simmer 5 minutes.

3. Cut polenta roll into 9 slices and arrange in greased 9-inch square casserole. Top with sausage mixture. Bake for 15 minutes or until heated through.   *Makes 4 servings*

Lasagna Supreme

8 ounces uncooked lasagna noodles
½ pound ground beef
½ pound mild Italian sausage, casings removed
1 medium onion, chopped
2 cloves garlic, minced
1 can (14½ ounces) whole peeled tomatoes, undrained and chopped
1 can (6 ounces) tomato paste
2 teaspoons dried basil leaves
1 teaspoon dried marjoram leaves
1 can (4 ounces) sliced mushrooms, drained
2 eggs
2 cups (16 ounces) cream-style cottage cheese
¾ cup grated Parmesan cheese, divided
2 tablespoons dried parsley flakes
½ teaspoon salt
½ teaspoon black pepper
2 cups (8 ounces) shredded Cheddar cheese
3 cups (12 ounces) shredded mozzarella cheese

1. Cook lasagna noodles according to package directions; drain.

2. Cook meats, onion and garlic in large skillet over medium-high heat until meat is brown, stirring to separate meat. Drain drippings from skillet.

3. Add tomatoes with juice, tomato paste, basil and marjoram. Reduce heat to low. Cover; simmer 15 minutes, stirring often. Stir in mushrooms; set aside.

4. Preheat oven to 375°F. Beat eggs in large bowl; add cottage cheese, ½ cup Parmesan cheese, parsley, salt and pepper. Mix well.

5. Place half the noodles in bottom of greased 13×9-inch baking pan. Spread half the cottage cheese mixture over noodles, then half the meat mixture and half the Cheddar cheese and mozzarella cheese. Repeat layers. Sprinkle with remaining ¼ cup Parmesan cheese.

6. Bake lasagna 40 to 45 minutes or until bubbly. Let stand 10 minutes before cutting.

Makes 8 to 10 servings

Note: Lasagna may be assembled, covered and refrigerated up to 2 days in advance. Bake, uncovered, in preheated 375°F oven 60 minutes or until bubbly.

Lasagna Supreme

32

Hungarian Goulash Casserole

1 pound ground pork
¼ teaspoon salt
¼ teaspoon black pepper
¼ teaspoon ground nutmeg
1 tablespoon vegetable oil
1 cup reduced-fat sour cream, divided
1 tablespoon cornstarch
1 can (10¾ ounces) cream of celery soup
1 cup milk
1 teaspoon sweet Hungarian paprika
1 package (12 ounces) egg noodles, cooked and drained
2 teaspoons minced fresh dill (optional)

1. Preheat oven to 325°F. Spray 13×9-inch casserole dish with nonstick cooking spray.

2. Combine pork, salt, pepper and nutmeg in bowl. Shape into 1-inch meatballs. Heat oil in large skillet over medium-high heat. Add meatballs. Cook 10 minutes or until browned on all sides and no longer pink in center. Remove meatballs from skillet; discard drippings.

3. Stir together ¼ cup sour cream and cornstarch in small bowl. Spoon into same skillet. Add remaining sour cream, soup, milk and paprika. Stir until smooth.

4. Spoon cooked noodles into prepared dish. Arrange meatballs over noodles and cover with sauce. Bake 20 minutes or until hot. Sprinkle with dill if desired. *Make 4 to 6 servings*

34

Hungarian Goulash Casserole

Veg•All® Beef & Cheddar Bake

2 cans (15 ounces each) VEG•ALL® Original Mixed Vegetables, drained
3 cups shredded Cheddar cheese
2 cups cooked elbow macaroni
1 pound extra-lean ground beef, cooked and drained
½ cup chopped onion
¼ teaspoon pepper

1. Preheat oven to 350°F.

2. In large mixing bowl, combine Veg•All, cheese, macaroni, ground beef, onion and pepper; mix well. Pour mixture into large casserole. Bake for 30 to 35 minutes. Serve hot.

Makes 4 to 6 servings

Old-Fashioned Beef Pot Pie

1 pound ground beef
1 can (11 ounces) condensed beef with vegetables and barley soup
½ cup water
1 package (10 ounces) frozen peas and carrots, thawed and drained
½ teaspoon seasoned salt
⅛ teaspoon garlic powder
⅛ teaspoon ground black pepper
1 cup (4 ounces) shredded Cheddar cheese, divided
1⅓ cups *French's*® French Fried Onions, divided
1 package (7½ ounces) refrigerated biscuits

Preheat oven to 350°F. In large skillet, brown ground beef in large chunks; drain. Stir in soup, water, vegetables and seasonings; bring to a boil. Reduce heat and simmer, uncovered, 5 minutes. Remove from heat; stir in ½ cup cheese and ⅔ *cup* French Fried Onions.

Pour mixture into 12×8-inch baking dish. Cut each biscuit in half; place, cut side down, around edge of casserole. Bake, uncovered, 15 to 20 minutes or until biscuits are done. Top with remaining cheese and ⅔ *cup* onions; bake, uncovered, 5 minutes or until onions are golden brown.

Makes 4 to 6 servings

Veg•All® Beef & Cheddar Bake

Easy Oven Beef Stew

2 pounds boneless beef stew meat, cut into 1½-inch cubes
1 can (16 ounces) tomatoes, undrained, cut up
1 can (10½ ounces) condensed beef broth
1 cup HOLLAND HOUSE® Red Cooking Wine
1 tablespoon dried Italian seasonings*
6 potatoes, peeled, quartered
6 carrots cut into 2-inch pieces
3 ribs celery cut into 1-inch pieces
2 medium onions, peeled, quartered
⅓ cup instant tapioca
¼ teaspoon black pepper
Chopped fresh parsley

*You may substitute 1½ teaspoons each of dried basil and oregano for Italian seasonings.

Heat oven to 325°F. Combine all ingredients except parsley in ovenproof Dutch oven; cover. Bake 2½ to 3 hours or until meat and vegetables are tender. Garnish with parsley.

Makes 8 servings

Spicy Lasagna Rollers

1½ pounds Italian sausage, casings removed
1 jar (28 ounces) spaghetti sauce, divided
1 can (8 ounces) tomato sauce
½ cup chopped roasted red pepper
¾ teaspoon dried Italian seasoning
½ teaspoon red pepper flakes
1 container (15 ounces) ricotta cheese
1 package (10 ounces) frozen chopped spinach, thawed and squeezed dry
2 cups (8 ounces) shredded Italian-blend cheese, divided
1 cup (4 ounces) shredded Cheddar cheese, divided
1 egg, lightly beaten
12 lasagna noodles, cooked and drained

Preheat oven to 350°F. Spray 13×9-inch baking pan with nonstick cooking spray; set aside.

Cook sausage in large skillet over medium heat until browned, stirring to break up meat; drain. Stir in ½ cup spaghetti sauce, tomato sauce, roasted pepper, Italian seasoning and pepper flakes.

Mix ricotta, spinach, 1½ cups Italian-blend cheese, ½ cup Cheddar cheese and egg in medium bowl. Spread ¼ cup ricotta mixture over each noodle. Top with ⅓ cup sausage mixture. Tightly roll up each noodle from short end, jelly-roll style. Place rolls, seam sides down, in prepared pan. Pour remaining spaghetti sauce over rolls. Sprinkle with remaining ½ cup Italian-blend cheese and ½ cup Cheddar cheese. Cover pan with foil.

Bake 30 minutes. Remove foil and bake 15 minutes or until sauce is bubbly.

Makes 6 servings

Zucchini Pasta Bake

1½ cups uncooked pasta tubes
½ pound ground beef
½ cup chopped onion
1 clove garlic, minced
Salt and pepper
1 can (14½ ounces) DEL MONTE® Zucchini with Italian-Style Tomato Sauce
1 teaspoon dried basil, crushed
1 cup (4 ounces) shredded Monterey Jack cheese

1. Cook pasta according to package directions; drain.

2. Cook beef with onion and garlic in large skillet; drain. Season with salt and pepper.

3. Stir in zucchini with tomato sauce and basil. Place pasta in 8-inch square baking dish. Top with meat mixture.

4. Bake at 350°F for 15 minutes. Top with cheese. Bake 3 minutes or until cheese is melted.

Makes 4 servings

Prep and Cook Time: 33 minutes

39

Mexi-Tortilla Casserole

1 tablespoon vegetable oil
1 small onion, chopped
1 pound ground pork*
1 can (14½ ounces) diced tomatoes, undrained
1 teaspoon dried oregano, crushed
¼ teaspoon salt
¼ teaspoon ground cumin
¼ teaspoon pepper
1½ cups (6 ounces) shredded Cheddar Jack with jalapeño peppers or taco-style cheese
2 cups tortilla chips
½ cup reduced-fat sour cream
1 can (4 ounces) diced green chilies, drained
2 tablespoons minced cilantro

*For a vegetarian casserole, substitute 1 pound tofu crumbles for the pork.

1. Preheat oven to 350°F.

2. Heat oil in large skillet. Add onion and cook 5 minutes or until tender. Add pork and cook until brown, breaking up with spoon. Pour off fat. Stir in tomatoes with juice, oregano, salt, cumin and pepper. Spoon into 11×7-inch casserole. Sprinkle cheese over casserole; arrange tortilla chips over cheese. Bake 10 to 15 minutes or until cheese melts.

3. Combine sour cream and chilies; mix until well blended. Drop by tablespoonfuls over baked casserole. Sprinkle with cilantro. *Makes 6 servings*

40

Cilantro is a green leafy herb that looks a lot like Italian parsley. Its distinctive flavor complements spicy foods, especially Mexican, Caribbean, Thai and Vietnamese dishes.

Mexi-Tortilla Casserole

Sweet and Savory Sausage Casserole

2 sweet potatoes, peeled and cut into 1-inch cubes
2 apples, peeled, cored and cut into 1-inch cubes
1 medium onion, cut into thin strips
2 tablespoons vegetable oil
2 teaspoons dried Italian seasoning
1 teaspoon garlic powder
½ teaspoon salt
½ teaspoon black pepper
1 pound cooked Italian sausage, cut into ½-inch pieces

Preheat oven to 400°F. Spray 13×9-inch baking pan with nonstick cooking spray.

Combine potatoes, apples, onion, oil, Italian seasoning, garlic powder, salt and pepper in large bowl. Toss to coat evenly. Place potato mixture into prepared pan. Bake, covered, 30 minutes. Add sausage to potato mixture; bake 5 to 10 minutes or until sausage is heated through and potatoes are tender.   *Makes 4 to 6 servings*

Creamy Beef and Vegetable Casserole

1 pound lean ground beef
1 small onion, chopped
1 bag (16 ounces) BIRDS EYE® frozen Farm Fresh Mixtures Broccoli, Corn & Red Peppers
1 can (10¾ ounces) cream of mushroom soup

• In medium skillet, brown beef and onion; drain excess fat.

• Meanwhile, in large saucepan, cook vegetables according to package directions; drain.

• Stir in beef mixture and soup. Cook over medium heat until heated through.
                                                    Makes 4 servings

Serving Suggestion: Serve over rice and sprinkle with ½ cup shredded Cheddar cheese.

Prep Time: 5 minutes
Cook Time: 10 to 15 minutes

Sweet and Savory Sausage Casserole

Quick Tamale Casserole

1½ pounds ground beef
¾ cup sliced green onions
1 can (4 ounces) chopped green chilies, drained and divided
1 can (16 ounces) whole kernel corn, drained
1 can (10¾ ounces) condensed tomato soup
¾ cup salsa
1 can (2¼ ounces) chopped pitted ripe olives (optional)
1 tablespoon Worcestershire sauce
1 teaspoon chili powder
¼ teaspoon garlic powder
4 slices (¾ ounce each) American cheese, halved
4 corn muffins, cut into ½-inch cubes
Mexican Sour Cream Topping (recipe follows, optional)

Preheat oven to 350°F. Brown ground beef with green onions in medium skillet over medium-high heat. Reserve 2 tablespoons chilies for Mexican Sour Cream Topping. Stir remaining chilies, corn, tomato soup, salsa, olives, Worcestershire sauce, chili powder and garlic powder into skillet until well blended. Place in 2-quart casserole. Top with cheese, then evenly spread muffin cubes over cheese. Bake 5 to 10 minutes or until cheese is melted. Meanwhile, prepare Mexican Sour Cream Topping. Serve casserole with topping, if desired.   *Makes 6 servings*

Mexican Sour Cream Topping

1 cup sour cream
2 tablespoons chopped green chilies, reserved from above
2 teaspoons chopped jalapeño peppers* (optional)
2 teaspoons lime juice

*Jalapeño peppers can sting and irritate the skin; wear rubber gloves when handling peppers and do not touch eyes. Wash hands after handling peppers.

Combine all ingredients in small bowl; mix until well blended.   *Makes about 1 cup*

Quick Tamale Casserole

Creamy SPAM™ Broccoli Casserole

Nonstick cooking spray
1 (7-ounce) package elbow macaroni
2 cups frozen cut broccoli, thawed and drained
1 (12-ounce) can SPAM® Lite, cubed
½ cup chopped red bell pepper
2 cups skim milk
2 tablespoons cornstarch
¼ teaspoon black pepper
1 cup (4 ounces) shredded fat-free Cheddar cheese
¾ cup soft bread crumbs
2 teaspoons margarine, melted

Heat oven to 350°F. Spray 2-quart casserole with nonstick cooking spray. Cook macaroni according to package directions; drain. In prepared casserole, combine macaroni, broccoli, SPAM® and bell pepper. In small saucepan, stir together milk, cornstarch and black pepper until cornstarch is dissolved. Bring to a boil, stirring constantly, until thickened. Reduce heat to low. Add cheese; stir until melted. Stir sauce into SPAM™ mixture. Combine bread crumbs and margarine; sprinkle on top of casserole. Bake 40 minutes or until thoroughly heated.

Makes 8 servings

46

To make soft bread crumbs, choose firm-textured bread and remove the crusts from five slices. Tear the bread slices into small pieces and place them in a food processor. Process using an on/off pulsing action until the crumbs are the desired size. If the bread is very soft, lightly toast it before tearing it into pieces.

Creamy SPAM™ Broccoli Casserole

Tuna Pot Pie

1 tablespoon margarine or butter
1 small onion, chopped
1 can (10¾ ounces) condensed cream of potato soup, undiluted
¼ cup milk
½ teaspoon dried thyme leaves
¼ teaspoon salt
⅛ teaspoon black pepper
2 cans (6 ounces each) albacore tuna in water, drained
1 package (16 ounces) frozen vegetable medley, such as broccoli, green beans, carrots and
    red peppers, thawed
2 tablespoons chopped fresh parsley
1 can (8 ounces) refrigerated crescent roll dough

1. Preheat oven to 350°F. Spray 11×7-inch baking dish with nonstick cooking spray.

2. Melt margarine in large skillet over medium heat. Add onion; cook and stir 2 minutes or until onion is tender. Add soup, milk, thyme, salt and pepper; cook and stir 3 to 4 minutes or until thick and bubbly. Stir in tuna, vegetables and parsley. Pour mixture into prepared dish.

3. Unroll crescent roll dough and divide into triangles. Place triangles over tuna filling without overlapping dough.

4. Bake, uncovered, 20 minutes or until triangles are golden brown. Let stand 5 minutes before serving.

Makes 6 servings

Note: Experiment with different vegetable combinations and create an exciting recipe every time. Just substitute a new medley for the one listed and enjoy the results.

Tuna Pot Pie

Rigatoni Con Ricotta

1 package (16 ounces) BARILLA® Rigatoni
2 eggs
1 container (15 ounces) ricotta cheese
¾ cup (3 ounces) grated Parmesan cheese
1 tablespoon dried parsley
2 jars (26 ounces each) BARILLA® Lasagna & Casserole Sauce or Marinara Pasta Sauce, divided
3 cups (12 ounces) shredded mozzarella cheese, divided

1. Preheat oven to 375°F. Spray 13×9×2-inch baking pan with nonstick cooking spray. Cook rigatoni according to package directions; drain.

2. Beat eggs in small bowl. Stir in ricotta, Parmesan and parsley.

3. To assemble casserole, spread 2 cups lasagna sauce to cover bottom of pan. Place half of cooked rigatoni over sauce; top with half of ricotta mixture, dropped by spoonfuls. Layer with 1 cup mozzarella, 2 cups lasagna sauce, remaining rigatoni and ricotta mixture. Top with 1 cup mozzarella, remaining lasagna sauce and remaining 1 cup mozzarella.

4. Cover with foil and bake 60 to 70 minutes or until bubbly. Uncover and continue cooking about 5 minutes or until cheese is melted. Let stand 15 minutes before serving.

Makes 12 servings

50

Traditional Italian ricotta cheese is not really a cheese at all, because it is not made from milk, but instead from whey, a by-product of the cheese making process. American manufacturers often make ricotta cheese from a combination of whey and milk.

Rigatoni Con Ricotta

Classic Stuffed Shells

1 jar (26 to 28 ounces) RAGÚ® Old World Style® Pasta Sauce, divided
2 pounds part-skim ricotta cheese
2 cups part-skim shredded mozzarella cheese (about 8 ounces)
¼ cup grated Parmesan cheese
3 eggs
1 tablespoon finely chopped fresh parsley
⅛ teaspoon ground black pepper
1 box (12 ounces) jumbo shells pasta, cooked and drained

Preheat oven to 350°F. In 13×9-inch baking pan, evenly spread 1 cup Ragú® Old World Style Pasta Sauce; set aside.

In large bowl, combine cheeses, eggs, parsley and black pepper. Fill shells with cheese mixture, then arrange in baking pan. Evenly top with remaining sauce. Bake 45 minutes or until sauce is bubbling.
Makes 8 servings

52

Cheesy Broccoli 'n Mushroom Bake

2 packages (10 ounces each) frozen broccoli spears, thawed
1 can (10¾ ounces) condensed cream of mushroom soup
½ cup MIRACLE WHIP® Salad Dressing
½ cup milk
1 cup KRAFT® Shredded Cheddar Cheese
½ cup coarsely crushed croutons

• ARRANGE broccoli in 12×8-inch baking dish.

• WHISK together soup, salad dressing and milk. Pour over broccoli. Sprinkle with cheese and croutons.

• BAKE at 350°F for 30 to 35 minutes or until thoroughly heated.   *Makes 6 to 8 servings*

Prep Time: 10 minutes
Bake Time: 35 minutes

Classic Stuffed Shells

Penne Tuna Casserole

1 package (16 ounces) uncooked BARILLA® Mini Penne
1 jar (26 ounces) BARILLA® Lasagna & Casserole Sauce
2 cans (6 ounces each) tuna, drained and separated into chunks
1½ cups shredded mozzarella cheese
3 tablespoons grated Parmesan cheese
Chopped parsley, for garnish

Preheat oven to 350°F.

Prepare penne according to package directions; drain.

Combine penne with BARILLA® sauce and tuna in 12×8-inch casserole and mix well. Sprinkle with cheeses and bake 40 minutes or until heated through and chesses are melted. Place casserole under broiler briefly to brown cheese, if desired. Garnish with chopped parsley, if desired. Serve immediately. *Makes 4 to 6 servings*

54

Wisconsin Cheese Pasta Casserole

1 pound spaghetti or fettuccine, broken into 3-inch pieces
1 quart prepared spaghetti sauce
½ cup plus ⅓ cup grated Wisconsin Romano cheese, divided
1¾ cups (7 ounces) sliced or shredded Wisconsin Colby cheese
1½ cups (6 ounces) shredded Wisconsin Mozzarella cheese

Prepare pasta according to package instructions: drain. Toss warm pasta with prepared spaghetti sauce to coat. Add ½ cup Romano cheese to mixture and mix well. Spread half of sauced pasta into bottom of a 13×9×2-inch baking dish. Cover with 1 cup of Colby cheese. Spread remaining pasta over cheese. Top with remaining ¾ cup Colby cheese. Sprinkle with remaining ⅓ cup Romano cheese and Mozzarella cheese. Bake at 350°F for 35 to 40 minutes or until top is lightly browned and casserole is bubbly. Remove from heat and let stand at least 10 minutes before serving. *Makes 6 to 8 servings*

*Favorite recipe from **Wisconsin Milk Marketing Board***

Veggie Pie with Cucina Classica™ Parmesan Cheese

  2 tablespoons olive oil
  2 large carrots, thinly sliced
  4 shallots, sliced or 2 bunches (about 15) scallions,* cut into ½-inch pieces
 15 fresh green beans,* cut in half
  6 eggs, beaten or equivalent egg substitute
  ½ cup low fat milk
  1 tablespoon all-purpose flour
  ½ teaspoon salt
  ⅛ teaspoon pepper
  ½ cup CUCINA CLASSICA™ Grated Parmesan cheese

*One-half cup peas can be substituted for green beans; medium yellow onion can be substituted for shallots.

Preheat oven to 350°F. Grease 9-inch square baking dish or 9-inch quiche pan. Set aside.

In large skillet, heat olive oil over medium heat. Add carrots, shallots and beans. Cook 5 minutes or until shallots are glossy and carrots and beans are tender-crisp, stirring occasionally. Drain off any excess oil.

In large mixing bowl, mix eggs, milk, flour, salt, pepper and Cucina Classica™ grated Parmesan cheese. Stir in vegetables. Pour into prepared baking dish. Bake 15 to 20 minutes or until set.

Makes 4 servings

55

Shallots belong to the same family as onions. Each shallot head is made up of two or three cloves, and each clove is covered in a papery skin that ranges in color from reddish tan to gold. The flesh is off-white with a hint of purple.

Tuna Noodle Casserole

7 ounces uncooked elbow macaroni
2 tablespoons margarine or butter
¾ cup chopped onion
½ cup thinly sliced celery
½ cup finely chopped red bell pepper
2 tablespoons all-purpose flour
1 teaspoon salt
⅛ teaspoon white pepper
1½ cups milk
1 can (6 ounces) albacore tuna in water, drained
½ cup grated Parmesan cheese, divided
Fresh dill sprigs (optional)

1. Preheat oven to 375°F. Spray 8-inch square baking dish with nonstick cooking spray.

2. Cook pasta according to package directions until al dente. Drain and set aside.

3. Meanwhile, melt margarine in large deep skillet over medium heat. Add onion; cook and stir 3 minutes. Add celery and bell pepper; cook and stir 3 minutes. Sprinkle flour, salt and white pepper over vegetables; cook and stir 1 minute. Gradually stir in milk; cook and stir until thickened. Remove from heat.

4. Add pasta, tuna and ¼ cup cheese to skillet; stir until pasta is well coated. Pour tuna mixture into prepared dish; sprinkle evenly with remaining ¼ cup cheese.

5. Bake, uncovered, 20 to 25 minutes or until hot and bubbly. Garnish with dill, if desired.

Makes 4 servings

Tuna Noodle Casserole

Cheesy Broccoli Bake

1 (10-ounce) package frozen chopped broccoli
1 (10¾-ounce) can condensed Cheddar cheese soup
½ cup sour cream
2 cups (12 ounces) chopped CURE 81® ham
2 cups cooked rice
½ cup soft, torn bread crumbs
1 tablespoon butter or margarine, melted

Heat oven to 350°F. Cook broccoli according to package directions; drain. Combine soup and sour cream. Stir in broccoli, ham and rice. Spoon into 1½-quart casserole. Combine bread crumbs and butter; sprinkle over casserole. Bake 30 to 35 minutes or until thoroughly heated.

Makes 4 to 6 servings

Pasta with Four Cheeses

¾ cup uncooked ziti or rigatoni
3 tablespoons butter, divided
½ cup grated CUCINA CLASSICA ITALIANA® Parmesan cheese, divided
¼ teaspoon ground nutmeg, divided
¼ cup GALBANI® Mascarpone
¾ cup (about 3½ ounces) shredded mozzarella cheese
¾ cup (about 3½ ounces) shredded BEL PAESE® semi-soft cheese

Preheat oven to 350°F. Lightly grease 1-quart casserole. Set aside.

In large saucepan of boiling water, cook pasta until tender but still firm. Drain in colander. Place in large mixing bowl. Stir in 1½ tablespoons butter, ¼ cup Parmesan cheese and ⅛ teaspoon nutmeg.

Spread one fourth of pasta mixture into prepared casserole. Spoon Mascarpone onto pasta. Layer with one fourth of pasta. Top with mozzarella. Add third layer of pasta. Sprinkle with Bel Paese® cheese. Top with remaining pasta. Dot with 1½ tablespoons butter. Sprinkle with remaining ¼ cup Parmesan cheese and ⅛ teaspoon nutmeg. Bake until golden brown, about 20 minutes.

Makes 4 servings

Cheesy Broccoli Bake

Grab a skillet, add a few ingredients and in no time you'll have a delicious meal that's sure to please the entire family—and cleanup is a breeze!

Chicken Enchilada Skillet Casserole

1 bag (16 ounces) BIRDS EYE® frozen Farm Fresh Mixtures Broccoli, Corn & Red Peppers
1 package (1¼ ounces) taco seasoning mix
1 can (16 ounces) diced tomatoes, undrained
3 cups shredded cooked chicken
1 cup shredded Monterey Jack cheese
8 ounces tortilla chips

- In large skillet, combine vegetables, seasoning mix, tomatoes and chicken; bring to boil over medium-high heat.

- Cover; cook 4 minutes or until vegetables are cooked and mixture is heated through.

- Sprinkle with cheese; cover and cook 2 minutes more or until cheese is melted.

- Serve with chips.   *Makes 4 servings*

Birds Eye Idea: Here's a quick lunch item for kids. Cut up 4 cooked hot dogs; stir into 1 bag of prepared Birds Eye® Pasta Secrets White Cheddar.

Prep Time: 5 minutes
Cook Time: 10 minutes

Chicken Enchilada Skillet Casserole

Curried Turkey and Couscous Skillet

1 tablespoon vegetable or olive oil
1 small onion, chopped
2 cloves garlic, minced
1 can (10½ ounces) kosher condensed chicken broth
⅓ cup water
2 teaspoons curry powder
¼ teaspoon ground red pepper
2 cups small broccoli flowerets
1 cup thinly sliced carrots
2 packages (4 ounces each) HEBREW NATIONAL® Sliced Oven Roasted Turkey Breast, cut
    into ½-inch strips
1 cup uncooked couscous
   Chopped fresh cilantro, for garnish

Heat oil in large deep nonstick skillet over medium heat. Add onion and garlic; cook 5 minutes or until onion is tender. Add broth, water, curry powder and ground red pepper to skillet; bring to a boil. Stir in broccoli and carrots. Cover; simmer 5 minutes or until vegetables are crisp-tender.

Stir turkey into broth mixture; cook until heated through. Stir in couscous, mixing well. Cover; remove from heat. Let stand 5 minutes or until liquid is absorbed. Garnish with cilantro, if desired.

Makes 4 servings

Couscous is coarsely ground durum wheat. It is a staple in North African cuisines. Most couscous available in the United States is precooked, which means it requires little or no cooking.

Curried Turkey and Couscous Skillet

Lemon-Garlic Chicken & Rice

4 skinless, boneless chicken breast halves
1 teaspoon paprika
  Salt and pepper (optional)
2 tablespoons margarine or butter
2 cloves garlic, minced
1 package (6.9 ounces) RICE-A-RONI® Chicken Flavor
1 tablespoon lemon juice
1 cup chopped red or green bell pepper
½ teaspoon grated lemon peel

1. Sprinkle chicken with paprika, salt and pepper.

2. In large skillet, melt margarine over medium-high heat. Add chicken and garlic; cook 2 minutes on each side or until browned. Remove from skillet; set aside, reserving drippings. Keep warm.

3. In same skillet, sauté rice-vermicelli mix in reserved drippings over medium heat until vermicelli is golden brown. Stir in 2¼ cups water, lemon juice and Special Seasonings. Top rice with chicken; bring to a boil over high heat.

4. Cover; reduce heat. Simmer 10 minutes. Stir in red pepper and lemon peel.

5. Cover; continue to simmer 10 minutes or until liquid is absorbed, rice is tender and chicken is no longer pink inside.
Makes 4 servings

64

Lemon-Garlic Chicken & Rice

Chicken Garden "Risotto"

2 boneless, skinless chicken breast halves
2 tablespoons CRISCO® Oil*
1 large sweet onion, finely chopped
1 tablespoon jarred minced garlic (or 2 large garlic cloves, peeled and minced)
1¾ cups (12 ounces) uncooked orzo pasta
2 cups broccoli flowerets, cut into bite-size pieces *or* 1 package (10½ ounces) frozen
    broccoli, thawed
2 cans (14½ ounces each) reduced-sodium chicken stock or broth
2 ears fresh corn, kernels cut from cobs *or* 1 package (10½ ounces) frozen corn, thawed
¼ teaspoon salt
¼ teaspoon freshly ground black pepper
¾ cup freshly grated Parmesan cheese

*Use your favorite Crisco Oil product.

1. Rinse chicken. Pat dry. Cut into 1-inch pieces.

2. Heat oil in 12-inch skillet on medium-high heat. Add onion and garlic. Cook 2 minutes. Add orzo, broccoli and broth. Reduce heat to medium. Cover skillet. Cook 6 minutes, stirring frequently. Add chicken. Cook 6 minutes. Mix in corn, salt and pepper. Cook 5 minutes.

3. Remove pan from heat. Stir in cheese gently. Serve hot.   *Makes 4 to 6 servings*

Note: Any combination of vegetables can be used, such as fresh or frozen peas, sliced carrots, sliced mushrooms, sliced zucchini or yellow squash.

Preparation Time: 20 minutes
Total Time: 35 minutes

Quick Chicken Jambalaya

8 boneless, skinless chicken thighs, cut in bite-size pieces
¼ teaspoon garlic salt
1 tablespoon vegetable oil
2½ cups 8-vegetable juice
1 bag (16 ounces) frozen pepper stir-fry mix
½ cup diced cooked ham
1 teaspoon hot pepper sauce
1¾ cups quick-cooking rice, uncooked

Sprinkle garlic salt over chicken. In large nonstick skillet, place oil and heat to medium-high temperature. Add chicken and cook, stirring occasionally, 8 minutes or until chicken is lightly browned. Add vegetable juice, pepper stir-fry mix, ham and hot pepper sauce. Heat to boiling; cover and cook over medium heat 4 minutes. Stir in rice; heat to boiling. Cover, remove pan from heat and let stand 5 minutes or until rice and vegetables are tender and liquid is absorbed. *Makes 4 servings*

*Favorite recipe from **Delmarva Poultry Industry, Inc.***

67

Italian-Style Chicken and Rice

1 tablespoon vegetable oil
4 boneless skinless chicken breasts (about 1 pound)
2 cups reduced-sodium chicken broth
1 box (about 6 ounces) chicken-flavored rice mix
½ cup chopped red bell pepper
½ cup frozen peas, thawed
¼ cup grated Romano cheese

1. Heat oil in large skillet. Add chicken; cook over medium-high heat 10 to 15 minutes or until lightly browned on both sides.

2. Add broth, rice mix, bell pepper and peas; mix well. Bring to a boil. Cover; reduce heat and simmer 10 minutes or until chicken is no longer pink in center. Remove from heat. Sprinkle with cheese; let stand covered 5 minutes or until liquid is absorbed. *Makes 4 servings*

Creole Chicken Thighs & Rice

2 tablespoons vegetable oil
2¼ pounds chicken thighs
½ teaspoon paprika
½ teaspoon dried thyme leaves
½ teaspoon salt
¼ teaspoon black pepper
½ cup chopped celery
½ cup chopped green bell pepper
½ cup chopped onion
2 cloves garlic, minced
1 cup long-grain or converted rice
1 can (14½ ounces) diced tomatoes, undrained
1 cup water
  Hot pepper sauce, to taste

68

Heat oil in large skillet or Dutch oven over medium heat until hot. Sprinkle chicken with paprika, thyme, salt and black pepper. Cook chicken 5 to 6 minutes on each side or until golden brown. Remove from skillet.

Add celery, bell pepper, onion and garlic to same skillet; cook 2 minutes. Add rice; cook 2 minutes, stirring to coat rice with oil. Stir in tomatoes with juice and water. Season with hot pepper sauce; bring to a boil.

Arrange chicken over rice mixture; reduce heat. Cover; simmer 20 minutes or until chicken is no longer pink in center and liquid is absorbed.

Makes 4 servings

Creole Chicken Thighs & Rice

Northwoods Mushroom Swiss Melt

4 TYSON® Individually Fresh Frozen® Boneless, Skinless Chicken Breasts
2 boxes UNCLE BEN'S® Long Grain & Wild Rice Original Recipe
3¾ cups water
½ cup chopped green bell pepper
½ cup chopped red bell pepper
1 cup sliced mushrooms
4 slices Swiss cheese

COOK: CLEAN: Wash hands. Remove protective ice glaze from frozen chicken by holding under cool running water 1 to 2 minutes. Spray large skillet with nonstick cooking spray. Add chicken; cook over medium-high heat 5 to 7 minutes or until light brown. Add water, rice and contents of seasoning packets. Bring to a boil. Cover, reduce heat; simmer 20 minutes. Stir in bell peppers; sprinkle mushrooms over chicken. Cook, covered, 5 to 8 minutes or until internal juices of chicken run clear. (Or insert instant-read meat thermometer in thickest part of chicken. Temperature should read 170°F.) Place cheese over chicken; remove from heat. Let stand, covered, 5 minutes or until cheese is melted.

SERVE: Serve chicken while still hot with rolls and mixed vegetables, if desired.

CHILL: Refrigerate leftovers immediately.   *Makes 4 servings*

Prep Time: none
Cook Time: 40 minutes

70

Northwoods Mushroom Swiss Melt

Simmered Tuscan Chicken

2 tablespoons olive or vegetable oil
1 pound boneless, skinless chicken breasts, cut into 1-inch cubes
2 cloves garlic, finely chopped
4 medium potatoes, cut into ½-inch cubes (about 4 cups)
1 medium red bell pepper, cut into large pieces
1 jar (26 to 28 ounces) RAGÚ® Old World Style® Pasta Sauce
1 pound fresh or frozen cut green beans
1 teaspoon dried basil leaves, crushed
   Salt and ground black pepper to taste

In 12-inch skillet, heat oil over medium-high heat and cook chicken with garlic until chicken is no longer pink. Remove chicken and set aside.

In same skillet, add potatoes and bell pepper. Cook over medium heat, stirring occasionally, 5 minutes. Stir in remaining ingredients. Bring to a boil over high heat. Reduce heat to low and simmer covered, stirring occasionally, 35 minutes or until potatoes are tender. Return chicken to skillet and heat through.   *Makes 6 servings*

Simmered Tuscan Chicken

Jiffy Chicken Supper

1 bag (16 ounces) BIRDS EYE® frozen Pasta Secrets White Cheddar or Creamy Peppercorn
¼ cup water
1 can (6½ ounces) chicken, drained
¼ cup pitted ripe olives, sliced
1 cup (8 ounces) plain yogurt
2 tablespoons chopped fresh parsley

• In large skillet, place Pasta Secrets and water. Bring to boil over high heat. Reduce heat to medium; cover and simmer 7 to 9 minutes or until pasta is tender.

• Stir in chicken and olives; cook 5 minutes more.

• In small bowl, combine yogurt and parsley.

• Stir yogurt mixture into Pasta Secrets mixture; cover and cook over low heat 1 minute or until heated through.   *Makes 4 servings*

Birds Eye Idea: To get a quick topping of crumbs for casseroles or skillets, rub two slices of toast together directly over the top. The crumbs will fall like magic!

Prep Time: 5 minutes
Cook Time: 15 to 18 minutes

Skillet Chicken Pot Pie

1 can (10¾ ounces) reduced-sodium cream of chicken soup
1¼ cups fat-free (skim) milk, divided
1 package (10 ounces) frozen mixed vegetables
2 cups diced cooked chicken
½ teaspoon black pepper
1 cup buttermilk biscuit baking mix
¼ teaspoon summer savory or parsley

1. Heat soup, 1 cup milk, vegetables, chicken and pepper in medium skillet over medium heat until mixture comes to a boil.

2. Meanwhile, combine biscuit mix and summer savory in small bowl. Stir in remaining 3 to 4 tablespoons milk just until soft batter is formed. Drop batter by tablespoonfuls onto chicken mixture to make 6 dumplings. Partially cover and simmer 12 minutes or until dumplings are cooked through, spooning liquid from pot pie over dumplings once or twice during cooking. Garnish with additional summer savory, if desired. *Makes 6 servings*

Prep and Cook Time: 25 minutes

One-Pot Chicken Couscous

   2 pounds boneless, skinless chicken breasts, cut into 1-inch chunks
   ¼ cup olive oil
   4 large carrots, peeled and sliced
   2 medium onions, diced
   2 large cloves garlic, minced
   2 cans (13¾ ounces each) chicken broth
   2 cups uncooked couscous
   2 teaspoons TABASCO® brand Pepper Sauce
   ½ teaspoon salt
   1 cup raisins or currants
   1 cup slivered almonds, toasted
   ¼ cup chopped fresh parsley or mint

Cook chicken in hot oil in 12-inch skillet over medium-high heat until well browned on all sides. With slotted spoon, remove chicken to plate. Reduce heat to medium. In remaining drippings cook carrots and onions 5 minutes. Add garlic; cook 2 minutes longer, stirring frequently.

Add chicken broth, couscous, TABASCO® Sauce, salt and chicken chunks. Heat to boiling, then reduce heat to low. Cover and simmer 5 minutes. Stir in raisins, almonds and parsley.
Makes 8 servings

75

Southern BBQ Chicken and Rice

1 cup UNCLE BEN'S® ORIGINAL CONVERTED® Brand Rice
4 TYSON® Individually Fresh Frozen® Chicken Half Breasts
1½ cups water
1 cup barbecue sauce, divided
1 package (6 half ears) frozen corn on the cob

COOK: CLEAN: Wash hands. In large skillet, combine water, rice, ¾ cup barbecue sauce and chicken. Bring to a boil. Cover, reduce heat; simmer 25 minutes. Add corn; cook 15 to 20 minutes or until internal juices of chicken run clear. (Or insert instant-read meat thermometer in thickest part of chicken. Temperature should read 170°F.) Spoon remaining ¼ cup barbecue sauce over chicken. Remove from heat; let stand 5 minutes or until liquid is absorbed.

SERVE: Serve with extra barbecue sauce and corn bread, if desired.

CHILL: Refrigerate leftovers immediately.   *Makes 4 servings*

76

Prep Time: none
Cook Time: 40 to 45 minutes

Skillet meals are ideal, easy-to-prepare recipes that include protein, starch and vegetables—an entire meal in one skillet. Cleanup is quick, too!

Southern BBQ Chicken and Rice

Curried Chicken with Couscous

1 package (5.7 ounces) curry flavor couscous mix
1 tablespoon butter or margarine
1 pound boneless skinless chicken breasts, cut into thin strips
½ bag (16 ounces) BIRDS EYE® frozen Farm Fresh Mixtures Broccoli, Cauliflower & Red Peppers
1⅓ cups water
½ cup raisins

• Remove seasoning packet from couscous mix; set aside.

• In large nonstick skillet, melt butter over medium-high heat. Add chicken; cook until browned on all sides.

• Stir in vegetables, water, raisins and seasoning packet; bring to boil. Reduce heat to medium-low; cover and simmer 5 minutes or until chicken is no longer pink in center.

• Stir in couscous; cover. Remove from heat; let stand 5 minutes. Stir before serving.

Makes 4 servings

78

Serving Suggestion: Serve with toasted pita bread rounds.

Birds Eye Idea: To add flavor to chicken breasts, simply rub them with lemon juice before cooking.

Prep Time: 5 minutes
Cook Time: 15 minutes

Curried Chicken with Couscous

Potato and Pork Frittata

12 ounces (about 3 cups) frozen hash brown potatoes
1 teaspoon Cajun seasoning
4 egg whites
2 whole eggs
¼ cup low-fat (1%) milk
1 teaspoon dry mustard
¼ teaspoon black pepper
10 ounces (about 3 cups) frozen stir-fry vegetable blend
⅓ cup water
¾ cup chopped cooked lean pork
½ cup (2 ounces) shredded Cheddar cheese

1. Preheat oven to 400°F. Spray baking sheet with nonstick cooking spray. Spread potatoes on baking sheet; sprinkle with Cajun seasoning. Bake 15 minutes or until hot. Remove from oven. *Reduce oven temperature to 350°F.*

2. Beat egg whites, eggs, milk, mustard and pepper in small bowl. Place vegetables and water in medium ovenproof nonstick skillet. Cook over medium heat 5 minutes or until vegetables are crisp-tender; drain.

3. Add pork and potatoes to vegetables in skillet; stir lightly. Add egg mixture. Sprinkle with cheese. Cook over medium-low heat 5 minutes. Place skillet in 350°F oven and bake 5 minutes or until egg mixture is set and cheese is melted. *Makes 4 servings*

Prep and Cook Time: 30 minutes

Helpful Hint

Two whole eggs may be substituted for the four egg whites, if desired.

80

Potato and Pork Frittata

Velveeta® Cheeseburger Mac

    1 pound ground beef
2¾ cups water
    ⅓ cup catsup
    1 to 2 teaspoons onion powder
    2 cups (8 ounces) elbow macaroni, uncooked
    ¾ pound (12 ounces) VELVEETA® Pasteurized Prepared Cheese Product, cut up

1. Brown meat in large skillet; drain.

2. Stir in water, catsup and onion powder. Bring to boil. Stir in macaroni. Reduce heat to medium-low; cover. Simmer 8 to 10 minutes or until macaroni is tender.

3. Add Velveeta; stir until melted.

Makes 4 to 6 servings

Safe Food Handling: Store ground beef in the coldest part of the refrigerator for up to 2 days. Make sure raw juices do not touch other foods. Ground meat can be wrapped airtight and frozen for up to 3 months.

Prep Time: 10 minutes
Cook Time: 15 minutes

82

French-American Rice

    ½ pound lean ground beef or ground turkey
    1 box (10 ounces) BIRDS EYE® frozen White and Wild Rice
1½ teaspoons soy sauce
    ½ cup California walnuts

- In large skillet, cook beef over medium-high heat 5 minutes or until well browned.

- Stir in rice; cook 5 minutes more or until rice is tender, stirring occasionally.

- Stir in soy sauce and California walnuts; cook 1 minute or until heated.

Makes 4 servings

Prep Time: 5 minutes
Cook Time: 10 minutes

Velveeta® Cheeseburger Mac

Pork Chops with Apples and Stuffing

4 pork chops, ½ inch thick
  Salt and pepper
1 tablespoon oil
2 medium apples, cored, cut into 8 wedges
1 cup apple juice
2 cups STOVE TOP® Cornbread Stuffing Mix in the Canister
¼ cup chopped pecans

SPRINKLE chops with salt and pepper. Heat oil in large skillet on medium-high heat. Add chops and apples; cook until chops are browned on both sides.

STIR in apple juice. Bring to a boil. Reduce heat to low; cover and simmer 8 minutes or until chops are cooked through. Remove chops from skillet.

STIR Stuffing Mix Pouch and pecans into skillet. Return chops to skillet; cover. Remove from heat. Let stand 5 minutes.   *Makes 4 servings*

Prep Time: 10 minutes
Cook Time: 20 minutes

84

Skillet Franks and Potatoes

3 tablespoons vegetable oil, divided
4 HEBREW NATIONAL® Quarter Pound Dinner Beef Franks or 4 Beef Knockwurst
3 cups chopped cooked red potatoes
1 cup chopped onion
1 cup chopped seeded green bell pepper or combination of green and red bell peppers
3 tablespoons chopped fresh parsley (optional)
1 teaspoon dried sage leaves
½ teaspoon salt
¼ teaspoon freshly ground black pepper

Heat 1 tablespoon oil in large nonstick skillet over medium heat. Score franks; add to skillet. Cook franks until browned. Transfer to plate; set aside.

Add remaining 2 tablespoons oil to skillet. Add potatoes, onion and bell pepper; cook and stir about 12 to 14 minutes or until potatoes are golden brown. Stir in parsley, sage, salt and black pepper.

Return franks to skillet; push down into potato mixture. Cook about 5 minutes or until heated through, turning once halfway through cooking time. *Makes 4 servings*

Spanish Rice and Meatballs

  6 slices bacon
  1 pound lean ground beef
  ½ cup soft bread crumbs
  1 egg, slightly beaten
  ½ teaspoon salt
  ⅛ teaspoon black pepper
  ½ cup chopped onion
  ½ cup sliced celery
  ⅔ cup uncooked white rice
 1½ cups water
  1 can (14½ ounces) whole peeled tomatoes, cut into bite-size pieces
  ⅓ cup HEINZ® 57 Sauce
  ¼ teaspoon black pepper
  ⅛ teaspoon hot pepper sauce
  1 green bell pepper, cut into ¾-inch chunks

In large skillet, cook bacon until crisp; remove, coarsely crumble and set aside. Drain drippings, reserving 1 tablespoon. In large bowl, combine beef, bread crumbs, egg, salt and ⅛ teaspoon black pepper. Form into 20 meatballs, using a rounded tablespoon for each. In same skillet, brown meatballs in reserved drippings; remove. In same skillet, sauté onion and celery until tender-crisp; drain excess fat. Add rice, water, tomatoes, 57 Sauce, ¼ teaspoon black pepper and hot pepper sauce. Cover; simmer 20 minutes. Stir in bacon, meatballs and bell pepper. Cover; simmer an additional 10 minutes or until rice is tender and liquid is absorbed, stirring occasionally. *Makes 4 servings (4 cups rice mixture)*

85

Sausage Ham Jambalaya

6 ounces spicy smoked sausage links, sliced
6 ounces cooked ham, diced
2 cans (14½ ounces each) DEL MONTE® Original Recipe Stewed Tomatoes
1 cup uncooked long grain white rice
1 large clove garlic, minced
1 tablespoon chopped fresh parsley
1 bay leaf

1. Brown sausage and ham in heavy 4-quart saucepan. Drain tomatoes, reserving liquid; pour liquid into measuring cup. Add water to measure 1½ cups.

2. Add reserved liquid, tomatoes and remaining ingredients to sausage mixture.

3. Cover and simmer 30 to 35 minutes, stirring occasionally. Remove bay leaf. Garnish with additional chopped parsley, if desired. *Makes 4 to 6 servings*

Prep Time: 10 minutes
Cook Time: 40 minutes

86

Beef Sonoma & Rice

1 pound lean ground beef (80% lean)
1 clove garlic, minced
1 package (6.8 ounces) RICE-A-RONI® Beef Flavor
½ cup chopped green bell pepper *or* 1 can (4 ounces) chopped green chiles, undrained
¼ cup sliced green onions
1 medium tomato, chopped
2 tablespoons chopped parsley or cilantro

1. In large skillet, brown ground beef and garlic; drain. Remove from skillet; set aside.

2. In same skillet, prepare Rice-A-Roni Mix as package directs, stirring in beef mixture, green pepper and onions during last 5 minutes of cooking.

3. Sprinkle with tomato and parsley. *Makes 4 servings*

Sausage Ham Jambalaya

Taco Pot Pie

  1 pound ground beef
  1 package (1¼ ounces) taco seasoning mix
  ¼ cup water
  1 can (8 ounces) kidney beans, rinsed and drained
  1 cup chopped tomato
  ¾ cup frozen corn, thawed
  ¾ cup frozen peas, thawed
1½ cups (6 ounces) shredded Cheddar cheese
  1 can (11½ ounces) refrigerated corn breadstick dough

1. Preheat oven to 400°F. Brown meat in medium ovenproof skillet over medium-high heat, stirring to separate; drain drippings. Add seasoning mix and water to skillet. Cook over medium-low heat 3 minutes or until most of liquid is absorbed, stirring occasionally.

2. Stir in beans, tomato, corn and peas. Cook 3 minutes or until mixture is hot. Remove from heat; stir in cheese.

3. Unwrap corn bread dough; separate into 16 strips. Twist strips, cutting to fit skillet. Arrange attractively over meat mixture. Press ends of dough lightly to edge of skillet to secure. Bake 15 minutes or until corn bread is golden brown and meat mixture is bubbly.

Makes 4 to 6 servings

Prep and Cook Time: 30 minutes

Taco Pot Pie

New Orleans Rice and Sausage

½ **pound smoked sausage,* cut into slices**
1 **can (14½ ounces) stewed tomatoes, Cajun- or Italian-style**
¾ **cup water**
1¾ **cups uncooked instant rice**
   Dash TABASCO® Pepper Sauce or to taste
1 **bag (16 ounces) BIRDS EYE® frozen Farm Fresh Mixtures Broccoli, Corn and Red Peppers**

*For a spicy dish, use andouille sausage. Any type of kielbasa or turkey kielbasa can also be used.

Heat sausage in large skillet 2 to 3 minutes.

Add tomatoes, water, rice and TABASCO® Pepper Sauce; mix well.

Add vegetables; mix well. Cover and cook over medium heat 5 to 7 minutes or until rice is tender and vegetables are heated through.   *Makes 6 servings*

Prep Time: 5 minutes
Cook Time: 10 minutes

90

Creamy Pasta Primavera

1 **bag (16 ounces) BIRDS EYE® frozen Pasta Secrets Primavera**
½ **cup 1% milk**
2 **packages (3 ounces each) cream cheese, cubed**
1 **cup cubed ham**
¼ **cup grated Parmesan cheese**

• In large skillet, heat Pasta Secrets in milk over medium heat to a simmer; cover and simmer 7 to 9 minutes or until vegetables are tender.

• Add cream cheese; reduce heat to low and cook until cream cheese is melted, stirring often.

• Stir in ham and cheese; cover and cook 5 minutes more.   *Makes 4 servings*

Prep Time: 10 minutes
Cook Time: 20 minutes

New Orleans Rice and Sausage

Velveeta® Cheesy Beef Stroganoff

1 pound ground beef
2 cups water
3 cups (6 ounces) medium egg noodles, uncooked
¾ pound (12 ounces) VELVEETA® Pasteurized Prepared Cheese Product, cut up
1 can (10¾ ounces) condensed cream of mushroom soup
¼ teaspoon black pepper

1. Brown meat in large skillet; drain.

2. Stir in water. Bring to boil. Stir in noodles. Reduce heat to medium-low; cover. Simmer 8 minutes or until noodles are tender.

3. Add Velveeta, soup and pepper; stir until Velveeta is melted.   *Makes 4 to 6 servings*

Prep Time: 10 minutes
Cook Time: 15 minutes

92

Velveeta® 15 Minute Cheesy Rice with Ham & Broccoli

2 cups cooked ham cut into strips
2 cups fresh or frozen broccoli flowerets, thawed
1 cup water
1½ cups MINUTE® White Rice, uncooked
½ pound (8 ounces) VELVEETA® Pasteurized Prepared Cheese Product, cut up

1. Bring ham, broccoli and water to boil in large skillet. Cover. Cook on medium heat 3 minutes.

2. Stir in rice and Velveeta; cover. Remove from heat. Let stand 7 minutes. Stir until Velveeta is melted.   *Makes 4 servings*

Velveeta® Cheesy Beef Stroganoff

Skillet Spaghetti and Sausage

¼ **pound mild or hot Italian sausage links, sliced**
½ **pound ground beef**
¼ **teaspoon dried oregano, crushed**
4 **ounces spaghetti, broken in half**
1 **can (14½ ounces) DEL MONTE® Diced Tomatoes with Basil, Garlic & Oregano**
1 **can (8 ounces) DEL MONTE Tomato Sauce**
1½ **cups sliced fresh mushrooms**
2 **stalks celery, sliced**

1. Brown sausage in large skillet over medium-high heat. Add beef and oregano; season to taste with salt and pepper, if desired.

2. Cook, stirring occasionally, until beef is browned; drain.

3. Add pasta, 1 cup water, undrained tomatoes, tomato sauce, mushrooms and celery. Bring to boil, stirring occasionally.

4. Reduce heat; cover and simmer 12 to 14 minutes or until spaghetti is tender. Garnish with grated Parmesan cheese and chopped parsley, if desired. Serve immediately.

Makes 4 to 6 servings

Prep Time: 5 minutes
Cook Time: 30 minutes

Easy Beef Stroganoff

2 **tablespoons oil**
2 **teaspoons finely chopped garlic**
½ **pound boneless sirloin steak, cut into thin strips**
¼ **cup dry red wine**
2 **teaspoons Worcestershire sauce**
1¼ **cups water**
½ **cup milk**
2 **tablespoons I CAN'T BELIEVE IT'S NOT BUTTER!® Spread**
1 **package LIPTON® Noodles & Sauce—Stroganoff**
½ **cup peeled pearl onions**

In 12-inch skillet, heat oil over medium heat and cook garlic 30 seconds. Add beef and cook over medium-high heat 1 minute or until almost done. Add wine and Worcestershire sauce and cook 30 seconds; remove beef.

Into skillet, stir water, milk, I Can't Believe It's Not Butter!® Spread and Noodles & Sauce—Stroganoff. Bring to the boiling point, then continue boiling, stirring occasionally, 7 minutes. Stir in onions and beef, then cook 2 minutes or until noodles are tender. Garnish, if desired, with chopped parsley and paprika.   *Makes about 2 servings*

Note: Recipe is also delicious with Lipton® Noodles & Sauce—Beef Flavor.

Easy Beef and Rice Stew

```
 2 tablespoons flour
½ teaspoon salt
¼ teaspoon pepper
 1 pound boneless beef top round, cut into ¾-inch chunks
 1 tablespoon oil
 2 medium carrots, diagonally sliced
 1 medium onion, coarsely chopped
 1 jar (4½ ounces) sliced mushrooms, drained
 1 can (14½ ounces) whole tomatoes, undrained, coarsely chopped
 1 can (10¼ ounces) beef gravy
¼ cup burgundy or other dry red wine
1½ cups MINUTE® Original Rice, uncooked
```

MIX flour, salt and pepper in large bowl. Add meat; toss to coat.

HEAT oil in large skillet on medium-high heat. Add meat; cook and stir until browned. Add carrots, onion and mushrooms; cook and stir 2 minutes.

STIR in tomatoes, gravy and wine. Bring to a boil. Reduce heat to low; cover and simmer 10 minutes.

STIR in rice; cover. Remove from heat. Let stand 5 minutes. Stir.   *Makes 4 servings*

Prep Time: 10 minutes
Cook Time: 20 minutes

95

Skillet Sausage and Bean Stew

   1 pound spicy Italian sausage, casing removed and sliced into ½-inch slices
   ½ onion, chopped
   2 cups frozen O'Brien-style potatoes with onions and peppers
   1 can (15 ounces) pinto beans, undrained
   1 teaspoon beef bouillon granules *or* 1 beef bouillon cube
   1 teaspoon dried oregano leaves
   ⅛ teaspoon ground red pepper

1. Combine sausage slices and onion in large nonstick skillet; cook and stir over medium-high heat 5 to 7 minutes or until meat is no longer pink. Drain drippings.

2. Stir in potatoes, beans, ¾ cup water, bouillon, oregano and red pepper; reduce heat to medium. Cover and simmer 15 minutes, stirring occasionally.   *Makes 4 servings*

Skillet Sausage and Peppers

   1 pound bulk Italian sausage
   1 medium onion, cut into wedges
   1 small green pepper, cut into strips
   1 small red pepper, cut into strips
   1 can (8 ounces) tomato sauce
   1 can (8 ounces) whole tomatoes, undrained
   ½ teaspoon dried oregano leaves
   2 cups STOVE TOP® Chicken Flavor Stuffing Mix in the Canister

BROWN sausage in large skillet on medium-high heat. Stir in onion, peppers, tomato sauce, tomatoes and oregano. Bring to boil. Reduce heat to low; cover and simmer 5 minutes or until vegetables are tender-crisp.

STIR in Stuffing Mix Pouch just to moisten; cover. Remove from heat. Let stand 5 minutes.

Makes 4 servings

Prep Time: 15 minutes
Cook Time: 15 minutes

Skillet Sausage and Bean Stew

Steak Hash

2 tablespoons vegetable oil
1 green bell pepper, chopped
½ medium onion, chopped
1 pound russet potatoes, baked and chopped
8 ounces cooked steak or roast beef, cut into 1-inch cubes
  Salt and black pepper, to taste
¼ cup (1 ounce) shredded Monterey Jack cheese
4 eggs

1. Heat oil in medium skillet over medium heat. Add bell pepper and onion; cook until tender. Stir in potatoes; reduce heat to low. Cover and cook, stirring occasionally, about 10 minutes or until potatoes are hot.

2. Stir in steak; season with salt and pepper. Sprinkle with cheese. Cover; cook about 5 minutes or until steak is hot and cheese is melted. Spoon onto 4 plates.

3. Meanwhile, prepare eggs as desired; top each serving with 1 egg.   *Makes 4 servings*

98

Chili with Rice

1 pound lean ground beef
2 cups water
1 can (15½ ounces) kidney beans, undrained
1 can (15 ounces) tomato sauce
1 package (1¾ ounces) chili seasoning mix
2 cups MINUTE® White Rice, uncooked
1 cup KRAFT® Shredded Cheddar Cheese

1. **BROWN** meat in large skillet on medium heat; drain.

2. **ADD** water, kidney beans, tomato sauce and seasoning mix. Bring to boil.

3. **STIR** in rice. Sprinkle with cheese; cover. Cook on low heat 5 minutes.   *Makes 6 servings*

Cook Time: 15 minutes

Steak Hash

Creamy Alfredo Seafood Newburg

2 tablespoons margarine or butter
¼ cup finely chopped onion
1 pound uncooked medium shrimp, peeled, deveined and coarsely chopped
1 jar (16 ounces) RAGÚ® Cheese Creations!® Classic Alfredo Sauce
¼ teaspoon ground white pepper
4 croissants or crescent rolls

1. In 12-inch nonstick skillet, melt margarine over medium-high heat and cook onion, stirring occasionally, 2 minutes or until tender.

2. Stir in shrimp and cook, stirring constantly, 2 minutes or until shrimp are almost pink. Stir in Ragú Cheese Creations! Sauce and pepper. Bring to a boil over high heat.

3. Reduce heat to low and simmer uncovered, stirring occasionally, 5 minutes or until shrimp turn pink. To serve, spoon shrimp mixture onto bottom of croissants and sprinkle, if desired, with chopped fresh parsley. Top with remaining croissant halves.   *Makes 4 servings*

100

Variation: For a light dish, substitute Ragú Cheese Creations! Light Parmesan Alfredo Sauce

Tip: Substitute 1 pound imitation crabmeat for shrimp.

Prep Time: 5 minutes
Cook Time: 15 minutes

This speedy version of Seafood Newburg is special enough to serve to dinner guests, but no one but you will know how easy it is to prepare.

Creamy Alfredo Seafood Newburg

Spicy Tuna and Linguine with Garlic and Pine Nuts

2 tablespoons olive oil
4 cloves garlic, minced
2 cups sliced mushrooms
½ cup chopped onion
½ teaspoon crushed red pepper
2½ cups chopped plum tomatoes
1 can (14½ ounces) chicken broth plus water to equal 2 cups
½ teaspoon salt
¼ teaspoon coarsely ground black pepper
1 package (9 ounces) uncooked fresh linguine
1 (7-ounce) pouch of STARKIST® Premium Albacore Tuna
⅓ cup chopped fresh cilantro
⅓ cup toasted pine nuts or almonds

102

In 12-inch skillet, heat olive oil over medium-high heat; sauté garlic, mushrooms, onion and red pepper until golden brown. Add tomatoes, chicken broth mixture, salt and black pepper; bring to a boil.

Separate uncooked linguine into strands; place in skillet and spoon sauce over. Reduce heat to simmer; cook, covered, 4 more minutes or until cooked through. Toss gently; add tuna and cilantro and toss again. Sprinkle with pine nuts.   *Makes 4 to 6 servings*

Do you know?

Since the process to extract pine nuts from pine cones is labor intensive, these Mediterranean nuts are expensive. Also known as pignoli or pignolia, pine nuts contain a high percentage of oil. To prevent them from spoiling, store them in the refrigerator for up to 3 months or in the freezer for up to 9 months

Spicy Tuna and Linguine with Garlic and Pine Nuts

Cheesy Deluxe Primavera Mac Skillet

2⅓ cups water
1 package (14 ounces) KRAFT® Light Deluxe Macaroni & Cheese Dinner
½ teaspoon dried basil leaves, crushed
½ teaspoon garlic powder
3 cups frozen vegetable medley (broccoli, cauliflower and carrots)

BRING water to boil in large skillet. Stir in Macaroni and seasonings; return to a boil.

STIR in vegetables. Reduce heat to medium-low; cover. Simmer 10 minutes or until macaroni is tender.

STIR in Cheese Sauce. Cook and stir 2 minutes on medium-high heat until thickened and creamy.   *Makes 5 servings*

Prep Time: 5 minutes
Cook Time: 15 minutes

104

Creole Shrimp and Rice

2 tablespoons olive oil
1 cup uncooked white rice
1 can (15 ounces) diced tomatoes with garlic, undrained
1½ cups water
1 teaspoon Creole or Cajun seasoning blend
1 pound peeled cooked medium shrimp
1 package (10 ounces) frozen okra *or* 1½ cups frozen sugar snap peas, thawed

1. Heat oil in large skillet over medium heat until hot. Add rice; cook and stir 2 to 3 minutes or until lightly browned.

2. Add tomatoes with juice, water and seasoning blend; bring to a boil. Reduce heat; cover and simmer 15 minutes.

3. Add shrimp and okra. Cook, covered, 3 minutes or until heated through.

Makes 4 servings

Cheesy Deluxe Primavera Mac Skillet

Tuna Veronique

2 leeks or green onions
½ cup thin carrot strips
1 stalk celery, cut diagonally into slices
1 tablespoon vegetable oil
1¾ cups *or* 1 can (14½ ounces) chicken broth
2 tablespoons cornstarch
⅓ cup dry white wine
1¼ cups seedless red and green grapes, cut into halves
1 (7-ounce) pouch of STARKIST® Premium Albacore or Chunk Light Tuna
1 tablespoon chopped chives
¼ teaspoon ground white or black pepper
4 to 5 slices bread, toasted and cut into quarters *or* 8 to 10 slices toasted French bread

If using leeks, wash thoroughly between leaves. Cut off white portion; trim and slice ¼ inch thick. Discard green portion. For green onions, trim and slice ¼ inch thick. In large nonstick skillet, sauté leeks, carrot and celery in oil for 3 minutes. In small bowl, stir together chicken broth and cornstarch until smooth; stir into vegetables. Cook and stir until mixture thickens and bubbles. Stir in wine; simmer 2 minutes. Stir in grapes, tuna, chives and pepper. Cook 2 minutes more to heat through. To serve, ladle sauce over toast.   *Makes 4 to 5 servings*

Prep Time: 20 minutes

Veronique is a French term used to describe dishes that include grapes as an ingredient or garnish.

Spicy Crabmeat Frittata

1 tablespoon olive oil
1 medium green bell pepper, finely chopped
2 cloves garlic, minced
6 eggs
1 can (6½ ounces) lump white crabmeat, drained
¼ teaspoon black pepper
¼ teaspoon salt
¼ teaspoon pepper sauce
1 large ripe plum tomato, seeded and finely chopped

1. Preheat broiler. Heat oil in 10-inch nonstick skillet with ovenproof handle over medium-high heat. Add bell pepper and garlic to skillet; cook and stir 3 minutes or until soft.

2. Meanwhile, beat eggs in medium bowl. Break up large pieces of crabmeat. Add crabmeat, black pepper, salt and pepper sauce to eggs; blend well. Set aside.

3. Add tomato to skillet, cook and stir for 1 minute. Add egg mixture. Reduce heat to medium-low; cook about 7 minutes or until eggs begin to set around edges.

4. Remove pan from burner and place under broiler 6 inches from heat. Broil about 2 minutes or until frittata is set and top is browned. Remove from broiler; slide frittata onto serving plate. Serve immediately. *Makes 4 servings*

Tip: Serve with crusty bread, cut-up raw vegetables and guacamole.

Prep & Cook Time: 20 minutes

Fresh crabmeat may be substituted for the canned crabmeat in this frittata. Purchase fresh crabmeat the day you plan to use it; store it in the coldest part of the refrigerator until you are ready to use it.

107

Thin Noodles with Chicken and Vegetables

6 ounces (about 3 cups) uncooked thin noodles or bean threads
½ cup chicken broth
2 tablespoons hoisin sauce
1 tablespoon vegetable oil
2 green onions, finely chopped
1 teaspoon minced fresh ginger
1 clove garlic, minced
1 pound boneless skinless chicken breasts, cut into bite-size pieces
1 package frozen vegetable medley,* thawed and drained
¼ cup orange marmalade
2 tablespoons chili sauce
¼ teaspoon red pepper flakes

*Use your favorite vegetable medley—for example, a medley of cauliflower, carrots and snow peas.

1. Place 6 cups water in wok or large saucepan; bring to a boil over high heat. Add noodles; cook 3 minutes or until *al dente,* stirring occasionally. Drain. Place noodles in medium bowl; stir in chicken broth and hoisin sauce. Set aside; keep warm.

2. Heat oil in wok or large skillet over high heat. Add onions, ginger and garlic; stir-fry 15 seconds. Add chicken; stir-fry 3 to 4 minutes. Add vegetables; stir-fry until vegetables are hot and chicken is no longer pink. Add marmalade, chili sauce and pepper flakes. Stir until hot. Serve over noodles.

Makes 4 servings

Get out the wok and stir-fry your way to a taste-tempting meal that just can't miss. Don't have a wok? That's okay, a large skillet will do.

Thin Noodles with Chicken and Vegetables

Chicken with Snow Peas

1½ pounds boneless skinless chicken breasts, cut into bite-size pieces
3 tablespoons light soy sauce
¼ cup all-purpose flour
2 tablespoons sugar
1 clove garlic, minced
½ teaspoon ground ginger
2 tablespoons vegetable oil
4 ounces shiitake or other fresh wild mushrooms, stemmed and cut into long thin strips
1 red bell pepper, cut into 1-inch triangles
4 ounces snow peas, trimmed
1½ cups chicken broth
1 tablespoon cornstarch
¼ teaspoon black pepper
Hot cooked rice

1. Combine chicken and soy sauce in medium bowl; cover and refrigerate 15 minutes to 1 hour.

2. Combine flour, sugar, garlic and ginger in pie plate. Drain chicken, reserving marinade. Roll chicken in flour mixture.

3. Heat oil in wok or large skillet over high heat. Add chicken; stir-fry 3 to 4 minutes or until no longer pink.

4. Add mushrooms; stir-fry 1 minute. Add bell pepper and snow peas; stir-fry 1 to 2 minutes or until crisp-tender.

5. Whisk together reserved marinade, chicken broth, cornstarch and black pepper in small bowl; add to chicken mixture in wok. Cook and stir until sauce boils; boil 1 minute. Transfer to serving platter. Serve with rice. Garnish with kale leaves, if desired.

Makes 5 to 6 servings

Chicken with Snow Peas

Southwest Chicken and Beans

3 tablespoons lemon juice
2 tablespoons seasoned stir-fry or hot oil, divided
2 tablespoons finely chopped onion
1 tablespoon white wine vinegar
1 clove garlic, minced
2 teaspoons chili powder
1 teaspoon salt
½ teaspoon dried oregano leaves
½ teaspoon ground cumin
½ teaspoon black pepper
1 pound boneless skinless chicken breasts or tenders, cut into ¼-inch strips
1 medium red onion, cut into thin strips
2 large red bell peppers, cut into ¼-inch strips
1 tablespoon minced cilantro
2 cans (16 ounces each) refried beans, warmed
   Tortilla chips, salsa and sour cream

112

1. Combine lemon juice, 1 tablespoon oil, chopped onion, vinegar, garlic, chili powder, salt, oregano, cumin and black pepper in medium bowl. Add chicken; toss to coat well. Cover and refrigerate 45 minutes to 8 hours.

2. Heat remaining 1 tablespoon oil in wok or large skillet over high heat. Add chicken mixture; stir-fry 3 minutes. Add onion strips; stir-fry 4 minutes. Add bell peppers; stir-fry 2 to 3 minutes or until vegetables are crisp-tender. Sprinkle with cilantro.

3. Serve chicken and vegetable mixture over beans with tortilla chips, salsa and sour cream on the side.   *Makes 4 to 5 servings*

Note: Seasoned stir-fry oils differ in "heat." If oil is too peppery, use 1 tablespoon vegetable oil and 1 tablespoon seasoned oil.

Southwest Chicken and Beans

Flash in the Pan Chicken & Veggie Stir-Fry

1½ pounds boneless skinless chicken, cut into 1-inch cubes
¼ cup teriyaki sauce
2 small zucchini, thinly sliced (about ¾ pound)
1 red or green bell pepper, cut into strips
1⅓ cups *French's®* French Fried Onions, divided
½ cup Italian salad dressing
1 teaspoon cornstarch

1. Toss chicken with teriyaki sauce. Heat 1 tablespoon oil in 12-inch nonstick skillet until hot. Stir-fry chicken 5 minutes or until browned. Add zucchini, pepper and ⅔ *cup* French Fried Onions; stir-fry 3 minutes or until vegetables are crisp-tender.

2. Combine dressing with cornstarch; stir into skillet. Heat to boiling. Cook 2 minutes or until sauce thickens. Sprinkle with remaining ⅔ *cup* onions.   *Makes 6 servings*

Prep Time: 10 minutes
Cook Time: 10 minutes

114

Quick Chicken Stir-Fry

½ cup MIRACLE WHIP® or MIRACLE WHIP LIGHT® Dressing, divided
4 boneless skinless chicken breast halves (about 1¼ pounds), cut into thin strips
¼ to ½ teaspoon garlic powder
1 package (16 ounces) frozen mixed vegetables *or* 3 cups fresh cut-up vegetables
2 tablespoons soy sauce
2 cups hot cooked MINUTE® White Rice

• Heat 2 tablespoons dressing in large skillet over medium-high heat. Add chicken and garlic powder; stir-fry 3 minutes.

• Add vegetables; stir-fry 3 minutes or until chicken is cooked through.

• Reduce heat to medium. Stir in remaining dressing and soy sauce; simmer 1 minute. Serve over rice.   *Makes 4 servings*

Prep Time: 10 minutes
Cook Time: 7 minutes

Stir-Fried Chicken with Broccoli

1 pound boneless skinless chicken tenders
2 tablespoons lemon juice
2 teaspoons grated lemon peel
1 teaspoon dried thyme leaves
½ teaspoon salt
¼ teaspoon ground white pepper
1 cup chicken broth
1 tablespoon cornstarch
3 tablespoons vegetable oil, divided
1 tablespoon butter
1 can (4 ounces) sliced mushrooms, drained
1 medium red onion, sliced
1 can (14 ounces) pre-cut baby corn*, rinsed and drained
2 cups frozen broccoli cuts, thawed
Hot cooked rice

*Or, substitute one (15-ounce) can whole baby corn, cut into 1-inch pieces.

1. Rinse chicken and pat dry with paper towels. Cut each chicken tender in half. Combine juice, lemon peel, thyme, salt and pepper in large bowl. Add chicken and toss to coat well. Marinate 10 minutes.

2. Stir broth into cornstarch in small bowl until smooth; set aside.

3. Heat wok over medium-high heat 1 minute or until hot. Drizzle 1 tablespoon oil into wok. Add butter and swirl to coat bottom; heat 30 seconds or until hot. Add mushrooms; stir-fry 1 minute. Add onion; stir-fry 2 minutes. Remove to large bowl.

4. Add remaining 2 tablespoons oil to wok and heat 1 minute or until hot. Add chicken in single layer; stir-fry 1½ minutes or until chicken is well browned on all sides and no longer pink in center. Remove to bowl with vegetable mixture.

5. Add corn to wok; stir-fry about 1 minute. Stir broth mixture until smooth; add to wok and cook until sauce boils and thickens. Add chicken mixture and broccoli; stir-fry until heated through. Serve over rice. *Makes 4 to 6 servings*

Note: Baby corn are tender miniature ears of corn that can be eaten cob and all. They're also great in soups and salads.

Oriental Chicken & Asparagus

6 TYSON® Fresh Boneless, Skinless Chicken Thighs
2 tablespoons cornstarch, divided
½ teaspoon salt
¼ pound fresh asparagus spears, trimmed and chopped
1 small red bell pepper, cut into thin strips
1 medium onion, sliced
2 tablespoons oyster sauce
1 clove garlic, minced
½ teaspoon sesame oil
1 can (14½ ounces) chicken broth
1 can (8 ounces) sliced water chestnuts, drained

PREP: CLEAN: Wash hands. Cut chicken into strips. CLEAN: Wash hands. Combine 1 tablespoon cornstarch and salt in medium bowl. Add chicken and stir to coat. Refrigerate.

COOK: Spray large nonstick skillet with nonstick cooking spray. Heat over medium-high heat. Cook and stir asparagus, bell pepper, onion, oyster sauce, garlic and oil about 3 minutes. Remove from pan. Cook and stir chicken about 5 minutes or until internal juices of chicken run clear. (Or insert instant-read meat thermometer in thickest part of chicken. Temperature should read 180°F.) Add broth and water chestnuts to skillet. Combine remaining 1 tablespoon cornstarch and ¼ cup water; add to skillet. Cook and stir until sauce is thickened. Return vegetables to skillet and heat through.

SERVE: Serve with cooked rice, if desired.

CHILL: Refrigerate leftovers immediately.

Makes 4 servings

Prep Time: 10 minutes
Cook Time: 20 minutes

116

Oriental Chicken & Asparagus

Lemon Chicken Herb Stir-Fry

1 tablespoon plus 1½ teaspoons peanut oil
2 green onions, cut into 1-inch pieces
1 large carrot, julienne cut
4 boneless, skinless chicken breast halves (about 1 pound), cut into strips
2 cups broccoli flowerettes
1 can (8 ounces) bamboo shoots, drained
1 cup LAWRY'S® Herb & Garlic Marinade with Lemon Juice
1 tablespoon soy sauce
½ teaspoon arrowroot
1 can (11 ounces) mandarin orange segments, drained (optional)
1 tablespoon sesame seeds
3 cups hot cooked rice

In large wok or skillet, heat oil. Add onion and carrot and cook over medium-high heat 5 minutes. Add chicken, broccoli and bamboo shoots; stir-fry 7 to 9 minutes until chicken is no longer pink in center and juices run clear when cut. In small bowl, combine Herb & Garlic Marinade with Lemon Juice, soy sauce and arrowroot; mix well. Add to skillet; continue cooking, stirring constantly, until sauce forms glaze. Stir in orange segments. Sprinkle with sesame seeds.

Makes 6 servings

Serving Suggestion: Serve over hot rice.

One pound boneless pork loin, cut into strips, may be subsituted for the chicken.

118

Lemon Chicken Herb Stir-Fry

Mandarin Orange Chicken

2 tablespoons rice vinegar
2 tablespoons light soy sauce
2 tablespoons olive oil, divided
2 teaspoons grated orange peel
1 clove garlic, minced
1 pound boneless skinless chicken breasts, cut into strips
2 cans (11 ounces each) mandarin oranges, undrained
½ cup (approximately) orange juice
2 tablespoons cornstarch
½ teaspoon red pepper flakes
1 onion, cut into thin wedges
1 small zucchini, cut into halves and sliced diagonally
1 small yellow squash, cut into halves and sliced diagonally
1 red bell pepper, cut into 1-inch triangles
1 can (3 ounces) chow mein noodles (optional)

120

1. Combine vinegar, soy sauce, 1 tablespoon oil, orange peel and garlic in medium bowl. Add chicken; toss to coat well. Cover and refrigerate 15 minutes to 1 hour.

2. Drain chicken, reserving marinade. Drain oranges, reserving liquid; set oranges aside. Combine marinade from chicken and liquid from oranges in small bowl; add enough orange juice to make 2 cups liquid. Whisk in cornstarch and red pepper flakes; set aside.

3. Heat remaining 1 tablespoon oil in wok or large skillet over high heat. Add chicken; stir-fry 2 to 3 minutes or until no longer pink. Remove chicken; set aside.

4. Stir-fry onion 1 minute over high heat. Add zucchini and squash; stir-fry 1 minute. Add bell pepper; stir-fry 1 minute or until all vegetables are crisp-tender. Add orange juice mixture. Cook and stir until mixture comes to a boil; boil 1 minute. Add chicken, cooking until hot. Add oranges and gently stir. Transfer to serving plate. Top with chow mein noodles, if desired.

Makes 6 servings

Mandarin Orange Chicken

Quick Oriental Feast

1 bag SUCCESS® Brown Rice
Vegetable cooking spray
½ pound skinless, boneless chicken breasts, cut into strips
2 cups sliced fresh mushrooms
1 package (10 ounces) frozen pea pods, thawed and drained
1 can (8 ounces) sliced water chestnuts, drained
6 green onions, chopped
2 teaspoons cornstarch
½ cup reduced-sodium chicken broth
2 teaspoons reduced-sodium soy sauce (optional)

Prepare rice according to package directions.

Spray large skillet with cooking spray. Add chicken; stir-fry over medium-high heat until chicken is no longer pink in center. Remove chicken from skillet; set aside. Spray skillet again with cooking spray. Add mushrooms, pea pods, water chestnuts and onions; stir-fry until tender. Combine cornstarch, chicken broth and soy sauce in small bowl; mix well. Return chicken to skillet. Add cornstarch mixture; cook and stir until sauce is thickened. Serve over hot rice.

Makes 4 servings

122

Bistro in a Pot

2 teaspoons Lucini Premium Select Extra Virgin Olive Oil
½ to 1 pound boneless skinless chicken, cut into bite-size pieces
½ cup minced shallots
2 large cloves garlic, sliced
2 cups chopped leeks, white and light green parts, washed and drained
1½ cups baby carrots, cut into quarters lengthwise
1 cup thinly sliced new potatoes
3 to 4 teaspoons dried lemon peel
2 tablespoons dried tarragon leaves
1 cup shredded JARLSBERG LITE™ cheese
1 cup frozen peas, thawed (optional)
Minced fresh parsley for garnish

In wok or large skillet with cover, heat olive oil over high heat until nearly smoking. Stir-fry chicken, shallots and garlic. Remove to bowl. Add leeks to wok and stir-fry 3 minutes. Add to chicken mixture. Add carrots, potatoes, lemon peel and tarragon to wok; stir-fry 5 minutes. Add chicken mixture to wok. Add ½ cup water; stir quickly. Cover tightly and steam 5 minutes. (Add more water if necessary.)

Remove from heat; add cheese and peas, if desired. Stir and serve.   *Makes 4 to 6 servings*

Serving Suggestion: Serve with a green salad and light sourdough French bread or crusty rolls.

Stir-Fried Pasta with Chicken 'n' Vegetables

6 ounces angel hair pasta, broken in thirds (about 3 cups)
¼ cup *Frank's® RedHot®* Cayenne Pepper Sauce
3 tablespoons soy sauce
2 teaspoons cornstarch
1 tablespoon sugar
½ teaspoon garlic powder
1 pound boneless skinless chicken, cut in ¾-inch cubes
1 package (16 ounces) frozen stir-fry vegetables

1. Cook pasta in boiling water until just tender. Drain. Combine **Frank's RedHot** Sauce, *¼ cup water,* soy sauce, cornstarch, sugar and garlic powder in small bowl; set aside.

2. Heat *1 tablespoon oil* in large nonstick skillet over high heat. Stir-fry chicken 3 minutes. Add vegetables; stir-fry 3 minutes or until crisp-tender. Add **Frank's RedHot** Sauce mixture. Heat to boiling. Reduce heat to medium-low. Cook, stirring, 1 to 2 minutes or until sauce is thickened.

3. Stir pasta into skillet; toss to coat evenly. Serve hot.   *Makes 4 servings*

Prep Time: 5 minutes
Cook Time: 15 minutes

123

Pad Thai

8 ounces uncooked rice noodles (⅛ inch wide)
2 tablespoons rice wine vinegar
1½ tablespoons fish sauce*
1 to 2 tablespoons fresh lemon juice
1 tablespoon ketchup
2 teaspoons sugar
¼ teaspoon red pepper flakes
1 tablespoon vegetable oil
4 ounces boneless skinless chicken breast, finely chopped
2 green onions, thinly sliced
2 cloves garlic, minced
2 cups fresh bean sprouts
3 ounces small shrimp, peeled
1 medium carrot, shredded
3 tablespoons minced fresh cilantro
2 tablespoons chopped unsalted dry-roasted peanuts

*Fish sauce is available at most larger supermarkets and Asian markets.

1. Place noodles in medium bowl. Cover with lukewarm water; let stand 30 minutes or until soft. Drain and set aside. Whisk rice wine vinegar, fish sauce, lemon juice, ketchup, sugar and red pepper flakes in small bowl; set aside.

2. Heat oil in wok or large nonstick skillet over medium-high heat. Add chicken, green onions and garlic. Cook and stir until chicken is no longer pink. Stir in noodles; cook 1 minute. Add bean sprouts and shrimp; cook just until shrimp turn opaque, about 3 minutes. Stir in fish sauce mixture; toss to coat evenly. Cook until heated through, about 2 minutes.

3. Arrange noodle mixture on platter; sprinkle with carrot, cilantro and peanuts. Garnish with lemon wedges, tomato wedges and additional fresh cilantro, if desired.   *Makes 5 servings*

Pad Thai

Almond Chicken

1½ cups water
4 tablespoons dry sherry, divided
4½ teaspoons plus 1 tablespoon cornstarch, divided
4 teaspoons soy sauce
1 teaspoon instant chicken bouillon granules
1 egg white
½ teaspoon salt
4 whole boneless skinless chicken breasts, cut into 1-inch pieces
Vegetable oil for frying
½ cup blanched whole almonds (about 3 ounces)
1 large carrot, diced
1 teaspoon minced fresh ginger
6 green onions, cut into 1-inch pieces
3 stalks celery, diagonally cut into ½-inch pieces
8 fresh mushrooms, sliced
½ cup sliced bamboo shoots (½ of 8-ounce can), drained

126

1. Combine water, 2 tablespoons sherry, 4½ teaspoons cornstarch, soy sauce and bouillon granules in small saucepan. Cook and stir over medium heat until mixture boils and thickens, about 5 minutes. Keep warm.

2. Combine remaining 2 tablespoons sherry, 1 tablespoon cornstarch, egg white and salt in medium bowl. Add chicken pieces; stir to coat well.

3. Heat oil in wok or large skillet over high heat to 375°F. Add half of the chicken pieces, one piece at a time, and cook 3 to 5 minutes until light brown and no longer pink. Drain on paper towels. Repeat with remaining chicken.

4. Remove all but 2 tablespoons oil from wok. Add almonds and stir-fry until golden, about 2 minutes; remove almonds and drain. Add carrot and ginger; stir-fry 1 minute. Add all remaining ingredients; stir-fry until crisp-tender, about 3 minutes. Stir in chicken, almonds and sauce; cook and stir until heated through.   *Makes 4 to 6 servings*

Almond Chicken

Shanghai Chicken Fried Rice

4 TYSON® Fresh or Individually Fresh Frozen® Boneless, Skinless Chicken Breasts
2 cups UNCLE BEN'S® Instant Rice
1 tablespoon peanut oil
1 teaspoon grated gingerroot *or* ¼ teaspoon ground ginger
1 package (16 ounces) frozen vegetables for stir-fry
¼ cup light teriyaki sauce
¼ cup chopped green onions

PREP: CLEAN: Wash hands. Remove protective ice glaze from frozen chicken by holding under cool running water 1 to 2 minutes. Cut chicken into 1-inch pieces. CLEAN: Wash hands.

COOK: Heat oil and gingerroot in large nonstick skillet; add chicken. Cook over medium-high heat until chicken is browned and internal juices run clear. (Or insert instant-read meat thermometer in thickest part of chicken. Temperature should read 170°F.) Stir in vegetables. Cook according to package directions. Meanwhile, prepare rice according to package directions. When vegetables are crisp-tender, stir in rice and teriyaki sauce. Cook until heated through. Sprinkle with green onions.

SERVE: Serve with egg rolls or hot and sour soup, if desired.

CHILL: Refrigerate leftovers immediately.   *Makes 4 servings*

Prep Time: 10 minutes
Cook Time: 20 minutes

128

Asian Chicken Stir-fry

2 tablespoons cornstarch
1 pound chicken breast tenders, cut into 4 crosswise pieces each
1 tablespoon peanut or canola oil
½ (16-ounce) bag ready-to-cook frozen mixed Asian vegetables
¼ cup teriyaki marinade
½ cup water
  Hot cooked rice

1. Place cornstarch and chicken pieces in plastic bag; shake well to coat.

2. Heat oil in 12-inch nonstick skillet over medium-high heat. Add vegetables; stir-fry until tender, 4 to 5 minutes.

3. Push vegetables to one side of pan. Add chicken pieces; stir-fry until no longer pink, about 4 minutes.

4. Add teriyaki marinade and water; bring to boil, stirring constantly, until sauce thickens.

5. Serve immediately over hot cooked rice.   *Makes 6 servings*

Quick Chicken Stir-Fry

4 TYSON® Fresh Boneless, Skinless Chicken Breasts
6 cups cooked UNCLE BEN'S NATURAL SELECT® Chicken & Herb Rice
1 clove garlic, minced
1 package (10 ounces) frozen broccoli, green beans, mushrooms and red peppers
1 medium onion, cut into wedges
⅓ cup shredded carrots
½ cup bottled hoisin sauce

PREP: CLEAN: Wash hands. Cut chicken into ¾-inch pieces. CLEAN: Wash hands.

COOK: Spray large nonstick skillet with nonstick cooking spray. Heat over medium-high heat. Add chicken and garlic; stir-fry 4 minutes. Add frozen vegetables, onion and carrots; stir-fry 3 minutes. Cover; cook 3 to 5 minutes or until vegetables are tender and internal juices of chicken run clear. (Or insert instant-read meat thermometer in thickest part of chicken. Temperature should read 170°F.) Stir in hoisin sauce. Heat thoroughly.

SERVE: Serve chicken and vegetables over hot cooked rice. Garnish with fresh cilantro, if desired.

CHILL: Refrigerate leftovers immediately.   *Makes 6 servings*

Prep Time: 10 minutes
Cook Time: 12 minutes

129

Cashew Chicken

10 ounces boneless skinless chicken breasts, cut into 1×½-inch pieces
1 tablespoon cornstarch
1 tablespoon dry white wine
1 tablespoon reduced-sodium soy sauce
½ teaspoon garlic powder
1 teaspoon vegetable oil
6 green onions, cut into 1-inch pieces
2 cups sliced mushrooms
1 red or green bell pepper, thinly sliced
1 can (6 ounces) sliced water chestnuts, rinsed and drained
2 tablespoons hoisin sauce (optional)
2 cups hot cooked white rice
¼ cup roasted cashews

1. Place chicken in large resealable plastic food storage bag. Blend cornstarch, wine, soy sauce and garlic powder in small bowl until smooth. Pour over chicken pieces. Seal bag; turn to coat. Marinate in refrigerator 1 hour. Drain chicken; discard marinade.

2. Heat oil in wok or large nonstick skillet over medium-high heat until hot. Add onions; stir-fry 1 minute. Add chicken; stir-fry 2 minutes or until browned. Add mushrooms, pepper and water chestnuts; stir-fry 3 minutes or until vegetables are crisp-tender and chicken is no longer pink in center. Stir in hoisin sauce; cook and stir 1 minute or until heated through.

3. Serve chicken and vegetables over rice. Top servings evenly with cashews. Serve immediately.   *Makes 4 servings*

130

Helpful Hint

Hoisin sauce is a traditional Chinese sauce made from soybean paste, garlic, chili peppers, vinegar, sugar and spices. It is sweet and slightly spicy. Store leftover hoisin sauce in a glass jar in the refrigerator—it keeps indefinitely.

Cashew Chicken

Santa Fe Spaghetti

8 ounces uncooked thin spaghetti or vermicelli
1 tablespoon vegetable oil
12 ounces boneless chicken or turkey, cut into strips
1½ teaspoons minced garlic
1 teaspoon ground cumin
1 teaspoon ground coriander
¼ teaspoon salt
⅛ teaspoon black pepper
1 package (16 ounces) frozen bell pepper and onion strips for stir-fry, thawed
1½ cups prepared salsa or picante sauce
½ cup sour cream
1½ teaspoons cornstarch
1 tablespoon chopped fresh cilantro or parsley

1. Cook spaghetti according to package directions.

2. Heat oil in large, deep skillet over medium-high heat until hot. Add chicken and garlic. Sprinkle with cumin, coriander, salt and black pepper; stir-fry 2 minutes.

3. Stir in bell peppers and onions and salsa; cook over medium heat 4 minutes. Combine sour cream and cornstarch in small bowl; mix well. Stir into chicken mixture; cook 2 to 3 minutes or until sauce has thickened and chicken is no longer pink in center, stirring occasionally.

4. Drain spaghetti; transfer to four serving plates. Top with chicken mixture; sprinkle with cilantro.   *Makes 4 servings*

Prep and Cook Time: 20 minutes

132

Santa Fe Spaghetti

Chicken with Walnuts

1 cup uncooked instant rice
½ cup chicken broth
¼ cup Chinese plum sauce
2 tablespoons soy sauce
2 teaspoons cornstarch
2 tablespoons vegetable oil, divided
3 cups frozen bell peppers and onions
1 pound boneless skinless chicken breasts, cut into ¼-inch slices
1 clove garlic, minced
1 cup walnut halves

1. Cook rice according to package directions.

2. Combine broth, plum sauce, soy sauce and cornstarch; set aside.

3. Heat 1 tablespoon oil in wok or large skillet over medium-high heat until hot. Add frozen peppers and onions; stir-fry 3 minutes or until crisp-tender. Remove vegetables from wok. Drain; discard liquid.

4. Heat remaining 1 tablespoon oil in same wok until hot. Add chicken and garlic; stir-fry 3 minutes or until chicken is no longer pink.

5. Stir broth mixture; add to wok. Cook and stir 1 minute or until sauce thickens. Stir in vegetables and walnuts; cook 1 minute more. Serve with rice.   *Makes 4 servings*

Lighten Up: To reduce sodium, use reduced-sodium chicken broth and reduced-sodium soy sauce. Omit or reduce salt when preparing rice.

Prep and Cook Time: 19 minutes

 *Helpful Hint*

Plum sauce is a thick Asian sauce made from plums and sometimes apricots, vinegar, chili peppers and spices. Once opened, plum sauce will keep up to one year in a tightly closed glass jar in the refrigerator.

Chicken & Broccoli Stir-Fry with Peanuts

1½ cups fat-free reduced-sodium chicken broth, divided
2 tablespoons reduced-sodium soy sauce
1½ tablespoons cornstarch
½ teaspoon salt
¼ teaspoon ground ginger
¼ teaspoon garlic powder
   Nonstick cooking spray
½ teaspoon vegetable oil
1 pound boneless skinless chicken breasts, cut into 2×¼-inch strips
1 cup small broccoli florets
1 cup red bell pepper strips
¼ cup chopped unsalted dry-roasted peanuts

1. Combine 1 cup chicken broth with soy sauce, cornstarch, salt, ginger and garlic powder in small container. Stir until smooth; set aside.

2. Lightly coat wok with cooking spray; heat over high heat until hot. Add oil; tilt wok to coat bottom. Add chicken; stir-fry 2 minutes or until no longer pink. Remove chicken from wok.

3. Add remaining ½ cup chicken broth to wok; bring to a boil. Add broccoli and bell pepper; return to a boil. Reduce heat and simmer, covered, 2 minutes or until broccoli is crisp-tender.

4. Increase heat to high. Add chicken. Stir cornstarch mixture and add to wok. Bring to a boil; boil 1 to 2 minutes or until thickened. Stir in peanuts.   *Makes 4 servings (1 cup each)*

135

You can reduce fat by using less oil in stir-fries. This recipe uses the technique of lightly coating the wok with cooking spray, heating it, then adding oil. The coating of cooking spray allows the small amount of oil to cling to the surface of the wok.

Quick 'n' Tangy Beef Stir-Fry

SAUCE
½ cup *French's*® **Worcestershire Sauce**
½ **cup water**
2 **tablespoons sugar**
2 **teaspoons cornstarch**
½ **teaspoon ground ginger**
½ **teaspoon garlic powder**

STIR-FRY
1 **pound thinly sliced beef steak**
3 **cups sliced bell peppers**

1. Combine ingredients for sauce. Marinate beef in ¼ *cup* sauce 5 minutes. Heat *1 tablespoon oil* in large skillet or wok over high heat. Stir-fry beef in batches 5 minutes or until browned.

2. Add peppers; cook 2 minutes. Add remaining sauce; stir-fry until sauce thickens. Serve over hot cooked rice or ramen noodles, if desired.   *Makes 4 servings*

Prep Time: 10 minutes
Cook Time: about 10 minutes

136

Sir-frying is a quick-cooking method in which pieces of meat and vegetables are cooked over high heat. To ensure even cooking and prevent burning, meat and vegetables should be stirred constantly. It is important to prepare all ingredients before beginning to cook.

Quick 'n' Tangy Beef Stir-Fry

Five-Spice Beef Stir-Fry

1 pound beef top sirloin, cut into thin strips
2 tablespoons reduced-sodium soy sauce
2 tablespoons plus 1½ teaspoons cornstarch, divided
3 tablespoons walnut or vegetable oil, divided
4 medium carrots, cut into matchstick-size pieces (about 2 cups)
1 red bell pepper, cut into chunks
1 yellow bell pepper, cut into chunks
1 cup chopped onion
¼ to ½ teaspoon red pepper flakes
1 tablespoon plus 1½ teaspoons packed dark brown sugar
2 teaspoons beef bouillon granules
1 teaspoon Chinese five-spice powder
3 cups hot cooked rice
½ cup honey-roasted peanuts

1. Place beef in shallow glass baking dish. Combine soy sauce and 2 tablespoons cornstarch in small bowl. Pour soy sauce mixture over beef; toss to coat thoroughly. Set aside.

2. Meanwhile, add 1 tablespoon oil to large nonstick skillet or wok. Heat skillet over high heat 1 minute or until hot. Add carrots. Stir-fry 3 to 4 minutes or until edges begin to brown. Remove carrots and set aside.

3. Reduce heat to medium-high. Add 1 tablespoon oil, bell peppers, onion and red pepper flakes; stir-fry 4 minutes or until onions are translucent. Remove vegetables and set aside separately from carrots.

4. Add remaining 1 tablespoon oil to skillet. Add beef; stir-fry 6 minutes.

5. Meanwhile, in small bowl, combine 1½ cups water with brown sugar, bouillon granules, five-spice powder and remaining 1½ teaspoons cornstarch. Stir until smooth.

6. Increase heat to high. Add bouillon mixture and reserved bell peppers and onions; bring to a boil. Cook and stir 2 to 3 minutes or until slightly thickened.

7. Toss rice with carrots; place on serving platter. Spoon beef mixture over rice and sprinkle peanuts over beef mixture.

Makes 4 servings

Five-Spice Beef Stir-Fry

Honey Dijon Beef and Vegetable Stir-Fry

⅔ cup HEINZ® Tomato Ketchup
2 tablespoons honey Dijon mustard
1 tablespoon soy sauce
1 pound boneless beef sirloin steak, cut into thin strips
1 red bell pepper, cut into thin strips
1 onion, cut into thin wedges
2 cups broccoli florets
  Hot cooked rice

In small bowl, combine ketchup, ⅓ cup water, mustard and soy sauce; set aside. In large preheated nonstick skillet, quickly brown beef; remove. Cook pepper, onion and broccoli, stirring, until crisp-tender, about 4 minutes. Return beef to skillet and stir in reserved ketchup mixture; heat. Serve with rice.   *Makes 4 servings*

140

Cantonese Sweet & Sour Pork

1 egg, well beaten
1 tablespoon cornstarch
1 tablespoon all-purpose flour
1 pound lean boneless pork, cut into 1-inch pieces
3 cups WESSON® Oil
1 teaspoon minced fresh garlic
1 teaspoon minced fresh gingerroot
1 green bell pepper, cut into 1-inch pieces
1 onion, cut into chunks
1 can (8 ounces) LA CHOY® Bamboo Shoots, drained
1 can (8 ounces) LA CHOY® Sliced Water Chestnuts, drained
2 jars (10 ounces each) LA CHOY® Sweet & Sour Sauce
2 teaspoons LA CHOY® Soy Sauce
  Hot cooked rice
1 can (5 ounces) LA CHOY® Chow Mein Noodles

In medium bowl, combine egg, cornstarch and flour. Add pork; toss gently. In large saucepan, heat oil to 350°F. Carefully add pork a few pieces at a time; deep-fry 3 minutes. Remove pork from oil; drain on paper towels. Let stand 5 minutes. Meanwhile, repeat with remaining pieces of pork. Return pork to hot oil; continue deep frying until golden brown. Remove pork from oil; drain again. Remove all but 2 tablespoons oil from saucepan. Add garlic and ginger to saucepan; cook and stir 30 seconds. Add green pepper and onion; stir-fry 2 minutes or until crisp-tender. Stir in all remaining ingredients except rice and noodles; bring to a boil. Return pork to saucepan; heat thoroughly, stirring occasionally. Serve over rice. Sprinkle with noodles.

Makes 4 to 6 servings

Broccoli Beef Stir-Fry

½ cup beef broth
4 tablespoons HOLLAND HOUSE® Sherry Cooking Wine, divided
2 tablespoons soy sauce
1 tablespoon cornstarch
1 teaspoon sugar
2 tablespoons vegetable oil, divided
2 cups fresh broccoli florets
1 cup fresh snow peas
1 red bell pepper, cut into strips
1 pound boneless top round or sirloin steak, slightly frozen, cut into thin strips
1 clove garlic, minced
4 cups hot cooked rice

1. To make sauce, in small bowl, combine broth, 2 tablespoons of cooking wine, soy sauce, cornstarch and sugar. Mix well and set aside. In large skillet or wok, heat 1 tablespoon oil. Stir-fry broccoli, snow peas and bell pepper 1 minute. Add remaining 2 tablespoons cooking wine.

2. Cover; cook 1 to 2 minutes. Remove from pan. Heat remaining 1 tablespoon oil; add meat and garlic. Stir-fry 5 minutes or until meat is browned. Add sauce to meat; cook 2 to 3 minutes or until thickened, stirring frequently. Add vegetables and heat through. Serve over cooked rice.

Makes 4 servings

141

Shredded Orange Beef

2 tablespoons soy sauce, divided
3 teaspoons cornstarch, divided
1½ teaspoons Asian sesame oil
1 egg white
1 small beef flank steak (about 1 pound), cut into strips
1 tablespoon sugar
1 tablespoon dry sherry
1 tablespoon white vinegar
2 cups vegetable oil
4 medium carrots, cut into julienne strips
2 tablespoons orange peel slivers
4 green onions with tops, cut into slivers
2 to 3 fresh red or green jalapeño peppers,* cut into strips
2 cloves garlic, minced

*Jalapeño peppers can sting and irritate the skin; wear rubber gloves when handling peppers and do not touch eyes. Wash hands after handling peppers.

142

1. Whisk together 1 tablespoon soy sauce, 1 teaspoon cornstarch, sesame oil and egg white in medium bowl. Add beef; toss to coat. Let beef marinate while preparing vegetables. Combine sugar, sherry, vinegar, remaining 1 tablespoon soy sauce and 2 teaspoons cornstarch in small bowl; mix well. Set aside.

2. Heat vegetable oil in wok over medium-high heat until oil registers 375°F on deep-fry thermometer. Add carrots and fry about 3 minutes or until tender. Remove carrots with slotted spoon and place in large strainer set over medium bowl. Reheat oil and fry orange peel about 15 seconds or until fragrant. Remove to paper towels; drain.

3. To double-fry beef,** add beef to wok; fry 1 minute or just until meat turns light in color. Remove beef to strainer placed over large bowl. Reheat oil to 375°F. Place ⅓ of drained beef in oil and fry about 3 minutes or until browned. Transfer beef to strainer with carrots. Repeat with remaining beef in two batches, reheating oil to maintain temperature.

4. Pour off all oil from wok. Reheat wok over medium-high heat. Add onions, chilies and garlic; stir-fry 30 seconds. Stir cornstarch mixture and add to wok. Cook and stir until sauce thickens. Add beef, carrots and orange peel; stir-fry until hot.   *Makes 4 servings*

**This technique helps keep the meat moist inside and crispy on the outside. The first frying "seals" in the juices while the second frying cooks the meat until crisp.

Shredded Orange Beef

Orange Beef and Broccoli

1 pound lean boneless beef, cut 1 inch thick
½ cup orange juice
2 teaspoons reduced-sodium soy sauce
1 teaspoon sugar
3 teaspoons vegetable oil, divided
¾ pound broccoli, coarsely chopped
1 cup diagonally sliced carrots
½ cup thinly sliced red bell pepper
1 green onion, diagonally sliced
¾ cup cold water
2 teaspoons cornstarch
1 tablespoon grated orange peel
6 ounces uncooked yolk-free wide noodles

1. Slice beef across grain into ⅛-inch slices; place beef in nonmetallic bowl. Add orange juice, soy sauce and sugar; toss to coat evenly. Let stand 30 minutes, or cover and refrigerate overnight.

2. Heat 2 teaspoons oil in large nonstick skillet or wok over medium-high heat until hot. Add broccoli, carrots, bell pepper and green onion; cook and stir 2 minutes. Remove vegetables to large bowl.

3. Drain beef; reserve marinade. Heat remaining 1 teaspoon oil in same skillet over medium-high heat until hot. Add beef to skillet; cook 1 to 2 minutes or until no longer pink. Add vegetables and reserved marinade to skillet; bring to a boil. Stir water into cornstarch until smooth; add to skillet. Cook until thickened, stirring constantly. Sprinkle with grated orange peel.

4. Cook noodles according to package directions, omitting salt; drain. Spoon beef mixture over noodles; serve immediately.

Makes 4 servings

144

Orange Beef and Broccoli

Stir-Fried Beef and Vegetables

⅔ cup beef broth or stock
2 tablespoons soy sauce
   Pinch of ground cinnamon
¼ teaspoon freshly ground black pepper
2 teaspoons cornstarch
2 tablespoons cold water
3 tablespoons CRISCO® Oil*
1 tablespoon chopped fresh ginger
2 teaspoons minced garlic *or* 1 large garlic clove, peeled and minced
1 pound lean beef, such as flank steak or boneless sirloin, trimmed and cut into
   ¼-inch-thick slices
1 carrot, peeled and thinly sliced
1 bunch scallions (or green onions), trimmed and cut into 1-inch pieces
¼ pound fresh snow peas, rinsed and stems removed

*Use your favorite Crisco Oil product.

146

1. Combine broth, soy sauce, cinnamon and pepper in small bowl. Set aside. Combine cornstarch and water in small bowl. Stir to dissolve.

2. Heat oil in wok or large skillet on medium-high heat. Add ginger and garlic. Stir-fry 30 seconds. Add beef, carrot and scallions. Stir-fry 3 minutes, or until beef is no longer red. Add broth mixture. Cook 2 minutes. Add snow peas. Cook 2 minutes, or until snow peas are bright green. Stir in cornstarch mixture. Cook 1 minute, or until thickened. Serve immediately.

Makes 4 servings

Note: Other vegetables can be used in place of those specified. Broccoli flowerets or sliced celery can be used in place of the carrot. Cooking time will be the same. In place of scallions, 1 medium onion, peeled and sliced, can be substituted. Fresh or frozen green peas can be used in place of snow peas.

Tip: If using canned broth, pour the remainder of the can into an ice cube tray and freeze. Once frozen, store the cubes in an air-tight plastic bag. That way you'll always have the few tablespoons of stock needed for many recipes.

Tip: It's easier to slice meat thinly if it's partially frozen. Wrap the steak in plastic wrap and freeze for 15 minutes. Always cut meat against the grain unless a recipe specifically says to slice it with the grain.

Preparation Time: 25 minutes
Total Time: 35 minutes

Vegetable Pork Stir-Fry

¾ **pound pork tenderloin**
1 **tablespoon vegetable oil**
1½ **cups (about 6 ounces) sliced fresh mushrooms**
1 **large green pepper, cut into strips**
1 **zucchini, thinly sliced**
2 **ribs celery, cut into diagonal slices**
1 **cup thinly sliced carrots**
1 **clove garlic, minced**
1 **cup chicken broth**
2 **tablespoons reduced-sodium soy sauce**
1½ **tablespoons cornstarch**
3 **cups hot cooked rice**

Slice pork across the grain into ⅛-inch strips. Brown pork strips in oil in large skillet over medium-high heat. Push meat to side of skillet. Add mushrooms, pepper, zucchini, celery, carrots and garlic; stir-fry about 3 minutes. Combine broth, soy sauce and cornstarch. Add to skillet and cook, stirring, until thickened; cook 1 minute longer. Serve over rice.

Makes 6 servings

*Favorite recipe from **USA Rice Federation***

Vegetables for stir-fries are sometimes cut on a diagonal. This increases the surface area that is in contact with the hot oil and shortens cooking time. Diagonal cuts also look attractive.

147

Cantonese Tomato Beef

2 tablespoons soy sauce
2 tablespoons Asian sesame oil, divided
1 tablespoon plus 1 teaspoon cornstarch, divided
1 small beef flank steak or filet mignon tail (about 1 pound), trimmed and
  cut into 2×¼-inch strips
1 pound fresh Chinese-style thin wheat noodles *or* 12 ounces uncooked spaghetti
1 cup beef broth
2 tablespoons brown sugar
1 tablespoon cider vinegar
2 tablespoons vegetable oil, divided
1 tablespoon minced fresh ginger
3 small onions (about 7 ounces), cut into wedges
2 pounds ripe tomatoes (5 large), cored and cut into wedges
1 green onion with tops, diagonally cut into thin slices
  Edible flowers, such as nasturtium, for garnish

148

1. Combine soy sauce, 1 tablespoon sesame oil and 1 teaspoon cornstarch in large bowl. Add beef strips; toss to coat. Set aside to marinate.

2. Cook noodles according to package directions just until tender. Combine beef broth, sugar, remaining 1 tablespoon cornstarch and vinegar in small bowl; mix until smooth. Set aside.

3. Drain cooked noodles in colander and return to stockpot. Add remaining 1 tablespoon sesame oil; toss. Keep warm.

4. Heat wok over high heat 1 minute or until hot. Drizzle 1 tablespoon vegetable oil into wok and heat 30 seconds. Add ginger and stir-fry about 30 seconds or until fragrant. Add beef mixture and stir-fry 5 minutes or until lightly browned. Remove beef to bowl and set aside. Reduce heat to medium.

5. Add remaining 1 tablespoon vegetable oil to wok. Add onion wedges; cook and stir about 2 minutes or until wilted. Stir in ½ of tomato wedges. Stir broth mixture and add to wok. Cook and stir until liquid boils and thickens.

6. Return beef and any juices to wok. Add remaining tomato wedges; cook and stir until heated through. Place cooked noodles in shallow serving bowl. Spoon tomato beef mixture over noodles. Sprinkle with green onion. Garnish, if desired. *Makes 4 servings*

Cantonese Tomato Beef

Green Dragon Stir-Fry

2 tablespoons vegetable oil, divided
1 pound beef flank steak, very thinly sliced
1 bunch asparagus *or* 8 ounces green beans, cut into 2-inch pieces
1 green bell pepper, cut into strips
1 cup julienne carrots
3 large green onions, sliced
1 tablespoon minced fresh ginger
1 clove garlic, minced
¼ cup water
1 tablespoon soy sauce
1 tablespoon TABASCO® brand Green Pepper Sauce
½ teaspoon salt
2 cups hot cooked rice (optional)

Heat 1 tablespoon oil in 12-inch skillet over medium-high heat. Add flank steak; cook until well browned on all sides, stirring frequently. Remove steak to plate with slotted spoon.

Heat remaining 1 tablespoon oil in skillet over medium heat. Add asparagus, green bell pepper, carrots, green onions, ginger and garlic; cook about 3 minutes, stirring frequently. Add water, soy sauce, TABASCO® Green Pepper Sauce, salt and steak; heat to boiling over high heat.

Reduce heat to low; simmer, uncovered, 3 minutes, stirring occasionally. Serve with rice, if desired.   *Makes 4 servings*

Note: Stir-fry is also delicious served over ramen or soba noodles.

Green Dragon Stir-Fry

Jambalaya Stir-Fry on Cajun Rice

1¾ cups water
1 cup uncooked converted rice
1 can (16 ounces) diced tomatoes, undrained
½ cup finely chopped celery
2 teaspoons chicken bouillon granules
1 bay leaf
8 ounces andouille sausage, cut into ¼-inch rounds*
1½ cups chopped onions
1 cup chopped green bell pepper
½ pound raw large shrimp, peeled and deveined
½ pound boneless chicken breasts, cut into 1-inch pieces
¾ teaspoon dried thyme leaves
¼ cup chopped fresh parsley
1 teaspoon salt
½ teaspoon ground red pepper
½ teaspoon paprika
Hot pepper sauce

*If andouille sausage is not available, use kielbasa sausage.

1. Bring water to a boil in medium saucepan. Add rice, tomatoes with juice, celery, bouillon granules and bay leaf. Return to a boil; reduce heat, cover tightly and simmer 20 minutes or until all liquid is absorbed. Remove and discard bay leaf.

2. Meanwhile, heat large skillet over medium-high heat 1 minute. Add sausage, onions and bell pepper; cook and stir 10 minutes.

3. Increase heat to high; add shrimp, chicken and thyme. Cook and stir 5 minutes. Add parsley, salt, ground red pepper and paprika. Stir to blend thoroughly.

4. Place rice on platter. Spoon shrimp mixture over rice and serve with pepper sauce.

Makes 4 servings

Jambalaya Stir-Fry on Cajun Rice

Ginger Beef & Noodle Stir-Fry

1 pound flank steak, cut into thin strips
½ cup LAWRY'S® Thai Ginger Marinade with Lime Juice
1 tablespoon vegetable oil
2 cups broccoli florettes
1 red bell pepper, chopped
2 tablespoons soy sauce
1 teaspoon cornstarch
1 teaspoon LAWRY'S® Garlic Powder with Parsley
1 package (7 ounces) chuka soba noodles (Japanese-style noodles) prepared according to package directions

In large resealable plastic food storage bag, combine beef and Thai Ginger Marinade with Lime Juice; seal bag. Marinate in refrigerator at least 30 minutes. In large skillet, heat oil. Add broccoli and bell pepper. Stir-Fry over high heat 2 minutes; remove and set aside. Remove steak; discard used marinade. In same skillet cook beef over high heat about 5 to 7 minutes. In small bowl combine soy sauce, cornstarch and Garlic Powder with Parsley; mix well. Add to beef; cook over medium heat until sauce is thickened. Stir in broccoli and bell pepper; heat through. Spoon over noodles.

Makes 4 servings

Serving Suggestion: Serve with flat rice crackers.

Hint: Vermicelli noodles may be substituted for chuka soba noodles.

Marinating adds flavor to meat. If the marinade contains an acidic ingredient, such as citrus juice or vinegar, it will also tenderize meat. It is best to marinate meat in the refrigerator rather than at room temperature.

Five-Spice Shrimp with Walnuts

1 pound medium or large raw shrimp, peeled and deveined
½ teaspoon Chinese five-spice powder
2 cloves garlic, minced
½ cup chicken broth
2 tablespoons soy sauce
2 tablespoons dry sherry
1 tablespoon cornstarch
1 tablespoon peanut or vegetable oil
1 large red bell pepper, cut into short, thin strips
⅓ cup walnut halves or quarters
   Hot cooked white rice (optional)
¼ cup thinly sliced green onions (optional)

1. Toss shrimp with five-spice powder and garlic in small bowl.

2. Blend broth, soy sauce and sherry into cornstarch in cup until smooth.

3. Heat wok or large skillet over medium-high heat. Add oil; heat until hot. Add shrimp mixture, bell pepper and walnuts; stir-fry 3 to 5 minutes until shrimp are opaque and bell pepper is crisp-tender.

4. Stir broth mixture and add to wok. Stir-fry 1 minute or until sauce boils and thickens. Serve over rice, if desired. Garnish with onions.   *Makes 4 servings*

155

Five spice powder is a mixture of ground cinnamon, cloves, star anise, fennel, Szechuan peppercorns and sometimes additional ingredients. It is used to flavor some Chinese dishes. It is available in Asian markets and large supermarkets.

If you think all chilis are alike, take a look at this varied collection. From the traditional beef-and-bean variety to chicken, sausage and meatless chilis, they're all here.

Chicken Chili

1 tablespoon vegetable oil
1 pound ground chicken or turkey
1 medium onion, chopped
1 medium green bell pepper, chopped
2 fresh jalapeño peppers,* chopped
1 can (28 ounces) tomatoes, cut up and undrained
1 can (15½ ounces) kidney beans, drained
1 can (8 ounces) tomato sauce
1 tablespoon chili powder
1 teaspoon salt
1 teaspoon dried oregano leaves
1 teaspoon ground cumin
¼ teaspoon ground red pepper
½ cup (2 ounces) shredded Cheddar cheese

*Jalapeño peppers can sting and irritate the skin; wear rubber gloves when handling peppers and do not touch eyes. Wash hands after handling.

Heat oil in 5-quart Dutch oven or large saucepan over medium-high heat. Cook chicken, onion and bell pepper until chicken is no longer pink and onion is crisp-tender, stirring frequently to break up chicken. Stir in jalapeño peppers, tomatoes with juice, beans, tomato sauce, chili powder, salt, oregano, cumin and red pepper. Bring to a boil over high heat. Reduce heat to medium-low; simmer, uncovered, 45 minutes to blend flavors. To serve, spoon into 6 bowls and top with cheese. *Makes 6 servings*

Chicken Chili

7-Spice Chili with Corn Bread Topping

1 pound ground turkey or lean beef
1 jar (16 ounces) Original or Spicy TABASCO® brand 7-Spice Chili Recipe
1 can (16 ounces) kidney beans, rinsed and drained
¾ cup water
1 package (12 ounces) corn muffin mix
1 can (7 ounces) whole kernel corn with sweet green and red peppers, drained
1 cup (4 ounces) shredded Cheddar cheese

In large skillet, brown turkey; drain. Stir in TABASCO® 7-Spice Chili Recipe, beans and water. Bring to a boil; reduce heat. Simmer 10 minutes.

Divide evenly among 6 (12-ounce) individual ramekins.

Meanwhile, prepare corn muffin mix according to package directions. Stir in corn and cheese until well blended.

Pour about ½ cup muffin mixture over top of each ramekin. Bake at 400°F 15 minutes or until corn bread topping is golden brown.   *Makes 6 servings*

Simple Turkey Chili

1 pound ground lean turkey
1 small onion, chopped
1 can (28 ounces) diced tomatoes, undrained
1 can (14 ounces) black beans
1 can (14 ounces) chick-peas, rinsed and drained
1 can (14 ounces) kidney beans, rinsed and drained
1 can (6 ounces) tomato sauce
1 can (4½ ounces) chopped mild green chilies
1 to 2 tablespoons chili powder, to taste

Cook turkey and onion in Dutch oven over medium-high heat until turkey is no longer pink, stirring with spoon to break up turkey; drain off fat. Stir in all remaining ingredients. Bring to a boil. Reduce heat and simmer, stirring occasionally, about 20 minutes.

Makes 8 servings

Southwest White Chili

SPICE BLEND
1 teaspoon McCORMICK® California Style Garlic Powder
1 teaspoon McCORMICK® Ground Cumin
½ teaspoon McCORMICK® Oregano Leaves
½ teaspoon McCORMICK® Cilantro Leaves
⅛ to ¼ teaspoon McCORMICK® Ground Red Pepper

CHILI
1 tablespoon olive oil
1½ pound boneless, skinless chicken breasts, cut into ½-inch cubes
¼ cup chopped onion
1 cup chicken broth
1 can (4 ounces) chopped green chilies, undrained
1 can (19 ounces) white kidney beans (cannellini), undrained
Shredded Monterey Jack cheese
Sliced scallions, for garnish

159

1. Place all ingredients for spice blend in small dish and stir until well blended. Set aside.

2. Heat oil in 2- to 3-quart saucepan over medium-high heat. Add chicken; cook and stir 4 to 5 minutes. Remove chicken with slotted spoon; cover and keep warm.

3. Add chopped onion to saucepan; cook and stir 2 minutes. Stir in chicken broth, chilies and reserved spice blend. Simmer over low heat 20 minutes.

4. Stir in beans and reserved chicken; simmer, uncovered, 10 minutes.

5. Spoon into serving dish and sprinkle with cheese and scallions.   *Makes 4 servings*

Serving Suggestion: For a quick accompaniment, whip up a batch of cornbread or corn muffins from a mix. For extra flavor, stir grated cheese, chopped scallions or jalapeño peppers or crisply cooked bacon into the batter.

White Bean Chili

Nonstick cooking spray
1 pound ground chicken
3 cups coarsely chopped celery
1½ cups coarsely chopped onions (about 2 medium)
3 cloves garlic, minced
4 teaspoons chili powder
1½ teaspoons ground cumin
¾ teaspoon ground allspice
¾ teaspoon ground cinnamon
½ teaspoon black pepper
1 can (16 ounces) whole tomatoes, coarsely chopped and undrained
1 can (15½ ounces) Great Northern beans, drained and rinsed
2 cups chicken broth

1. Spray large nonstick skillet with cooking spray; heat over medium heat until hot. Add chicken; cook and stir until browned, breaking into pieces with fork. Remove chicken; drain fat from skillet.

2. Add celery, onions and garlic to skillet; cook and stir over medium heat 5 to 7 minutes or until tender. Sprinkle with chili powder, cumin, allspice, cinnamon and pepper; cook and stir 1 minute.

3. Return chicken to skillet. Stir in tomatoes with juice, beans and chicken broth; heat to a boil. Reduce heat to low and simmer, uncovered, 15 minutes. Garnish as desired.

Makes 6 servings

Ground turkey may be substituted for the ground chicken in this recipe. If you wish to lower the amount of fat in the chili, choose a lean ground turkey product that is principally ground turkey breasts.

White Bean Chili

Vegetable-Beef Chili

1 (1-pound) beef top round or chuck steak, cut into ¼-inch cubes
1 tablespoon vegetable oil
1 cup coarsely chopped green bell pepper
½ cup coarsely chopped onion
1 clove garlic, minced
3 to 4 tablespoons chili powder
2 (16-ounce) cans tomatoes, undrained, coarsely chopped
¾ cup A.1.® Original or A.1.® BOLD & SPICY Steak Sauce
1 (17-ounce) can corn, drained
1 (15-ounce) can kidney beans, drained

Brown steak in oil in 6-quart pot over medium-high heat; drain if necessary. Reduce heat to medium; add pepper, onion and garlic. Cook and stir until vegetables are tender, about 3 minutes. Mix in chili powder; cook and stir 1 minute. Add tomatoes with liquid and steak sauce; heat to a boil.

Reduce heat. Cover; simmer 45 minutes, stirring occasionally. Add corn and beans; simmer 15 minutes more or until steak is tender. Serve immediately. Garnish as desired.

Makes 6 servings

Hearty Chili

2 pounds BOB EVANS® Original Recipe Roll Sausage
1½ cups chopped onions
1 (1¼-ounce) package chili seasoning
3 cups tomato sauce
3 cups tomato juice
1 (30-ounce) can chili or kidney beans
Hot pepper sauce to taste (optional)

Crumble sausage into large Dutch oven. Add onions. Cook over medium heat until sausage is browned, stirring occasionally. Drain off any drippings; stir in seasoning, then remaining ingredients. Bring to a boil over high heat. Reduce heat to low; simmer, uncovered, 30 minutes. Serve hot. Refrigerate leftovers.

Makes 8 servings

Vegetable-Beef Chili

30-Minute Chili Olé

1 cup chopped onion
2 cloves garlic, minced
1 tablespoon vegetable oil
2 pounds ground beef
1 (15-ounce) can tomato sauce
1 (14½-ounce) can stewed tomatoes
¾ cup A.1.® Steak Sauce
1 tablespoon chili powder
1 teaspoon ground cumin
1 (16-ounce) can black beans, rinsed and drained
1 (11-ounce) can corn, drained
   Shredded cheese, sour cream and chopped tomato, for garnish

Sauté onion and garlic in oil in 6-quart heavy pot over medium-high heat until tender.

Add beef; cook and stir until brown. Drain; stir in tomato sauce, stewed tomatoes, steak sauce, chili powder and cumin.

Heat to a boil; reduce heat to low. Cover; simmer for 10 minutes, stirring occasionally. Stir in beans and corn; simmer, uncovered, for 10 minutes.

Serve hot, garnished with cheese, sour cream and tomatoes.   *Makes 8 servings*

164

Kahlúa® Turkey Chili Verde

3½ pounds turkey thighs
¼ cup olive oil
2 medium onions, chopped
12 large cloves garlic, peeled and chopped
1 large green bell pepper, chopped
2 tablespoons all-purpose flour
1 (28-ounce) can Italian tomatoes, drained and chopped
1 (14½-ounce) can chicken broth
1 (13-ounce) can tomatillos,* drained and mashed
1½ cups chopped cilantro
4 (7-ounce) cans diced mild green chilies
½ cup KAHLÚA® Liqueur
2 jalapeño chilies, diced**
5 teaspoons dried oregano leaves
2 teaspoons ground coriander seeds
2 teaspoons ground cumin
   Salt, freshly ground black pepper and fresh lime juice

*Tomatillos (Mexican green tomatoes) can be found in the ethnic section of large supermarkets.

**Jalapeno chilies can sting and irritate the skin; wear rubber gloves when handling chilies and do not touch eyes. Wash hands after handling chilies.

In large skillet, brown turkey thighs in olive oil over high heat, turning occasionally, about 15 minutes. Transfer to large roasting pan. Set aside. Discard all but ¼ cup drippings in skillet. Add onions, garlic and bell pepper; cook over medium heat until soft, about 10 minutes, stirring frequently. Add flour; cook and stir 3 to 4 minutes. Stir in tomatoes, chicken broth, tomatillos, cilantro, green chilies, Kahlúa®, jalapeño chilies, oregano, coriander and cumin. Bring to boil. Pour over turkey thighs in roasting pan. Cover tightly with heavy-duty foil; bake at 350°F for 1 hour.

Remove from oven; loosen foil. Set turkey aside to cool. When cool enough to handle, remove skin and bones from turkey. Cut meat into ½-inch cubes and place in large saucepan with sauce. Cook over medium heat until heated through. Season to taste with salt, pepper and lime juice. Serve hot; garnish as desired. *Makes about 16 servings*

Sock-it-to-'em Chili

1 tablespoon vegetable oil
¾ pound ground turkey or lean ground beef
1 (8-ounce) package mushrooms, sliced
2 medium carrots, peeled and diced
1 large green bell pepper, seeded and diced
1 medium onion, diced
2 cloves garlic, minced
1½ teaspoons chili powder
½ teaspoon ground cumin
1 (26-ounce) jar NEWMAN'S OWN® Sockarooni Spaghetti Sauce
2 (15- to 19-ounce) cans black beans, undrained
1 cup water
1 medium zucchini, diced

Heat oil in 5-quart Dutch oven over medium-high heat until hot. Add turkey; cook and stir until no longer pink. Add mushrooms, carrots, bell pepper, onion, garlic, chili powder and cumin; cook until onion is tender, stirring frequently.

Stir in Newman's Own® Sockarooni Spaghetti Sauce, beans with their liquid and water; bring to a boil. Reduce heat to low; cover and simmer 20 minutes. Add zucchini; cook over medium-low heat, uncovered, 10 minutes or until zucchini is just tender. Serve hot.

Makes 6 servings

167

Steak and Black Bean Chili

¾ pound sirloin beef steak
1 teaspoon vegetable oil
1 cup chopped onion
2 cloves garlic, minced
2 cans (15 ounces each) black beans, rinsed and drained
1 can (15 ounces) diced tomatoes, undrained
1 cup chopped green bell pepper
1 cup chopped red bell pepper
1 jalapeño pepper,* minced
1 cube beef bouillon
2 tablespoons chili powder
½ teaspoon sugar
1 cup chopped tomato
⅔ cup sliced green onions with tops
6 tablespoons reduced-fat sour cream

168

*Jalapeño peppers can sting and irritate the skin; wear rubber gloves when handling peppers and do not touch eyes. Wash hands after handling peppers.

1. Trim fat from steak. Cut steak into ½-inch cubes. Heat oil in large nonstick saucepan over medium heat until hot. Add steak, onion and garlic; cook and stir 5 minutes or until meat is no longer pink. Add beans, diced tomatoes with juice, bell peppers, jalapeño pepper, bouillon, chili powder and sugar. Bring to a boil; reduce heat to low. Simmer, covered, 30 to 45 minutes.

2. Top with chopped tomato, green onions and sour cream.   *Makes 6 servings*

Steak and Black Bean Chili

Arizona Pork Chili

1 tablespoon vegetable oil
1½ pounds boneless pork, cut into ¼-inch cubes
   Salt and black pepper (optional)
1 can (15 ounces) black, pinto or kidney beans, drained
1 can (14½ ounces) DEL MONTE® Diced Tomatoes with Garlic & Onion, undrained
1 can (4 ounces) diced green chiles, drained
1 teaspoon ground cumin

1. Heat oil in large skillet over medium-high heat. Add pork; cook until browned. Season with salt and pepper to taste, if desired.

2. Add beans, tomatoes, chiles and cumin. Simmer 10 minutes, stirring occasionally. Serve with tortillas and sour cream, if desired. *Makes 6 servings*

Prep Time: 10 minutes
Cook Time: 25 minutes

170

Chunky Chili Con Carne

2 pounds ground beef
1 cup chopped onions
1 tablespoon minced fresh garlic
1 can (14.5 ounces) HUNT'S® Whole Tomatoes
1 can (14.5 ounces) beef broth
1 can (6 ounces) HUNT'S® Tomato Paste
3 tablespoons GEBHARDT® Chili Powder
1 teaspoon ground cumin
1 teaspoon salt
½ teaspoon *each:* dried oregano and cayenne pepper
1 can (30 ounces) chili beans

In large pot, brown meat with onions and garlic over medium heat; drain. Stir in tomatoes, broth, tomato paste, chili powder, cumin, salt, oregano and cayenne pepper; reduce heat to low and simmer 20 minutes. Stir in beans; simmer 10 minutes. *Makes 6 to 8 servings*

Arizona Pork Chili

Southern BBQ Chili

½ pound lean ground beef
1 medium onion, chopped
1 clove garlic, minced
1 can (14½ ounces) DEL MONTE® Diced Tomatoes with Green Pepper & Onion
¼ cup salsa
1 can (15 ounces) barbecue-style beans
1 can (15 ounces) black beans, drained
1 can (8¾ ounces) *or* 1 cup kidney beans, drained

1. Brown meat with onion and garlic in large saucepan; drain.

2. Add tomatoes, salsa and beans. Cover and simmer 15 minutes or until heated through. Top with sour cream and sliced green onions, if desired.　　　*Makes 6 servings*

Prep Time: 5 minutes
Cook Time: 20 minutes

172

Spicy Chili with Cornmeal Dumplings

1½ pounds ground beef
1¼ cups finely chopped green bell peppers
½ cup chopped onion
1 clove garlic, minced
½ cup A.1.® Original or A.1.® BOLD & SPICY Steak Sauce
3 large tomatoes, chopped (about 3½ cups)
1 (1¼-ounce) package taco seasoning mix
¼ teaspoon ground cumin
½ teaspoon crushed red pepper flakes
1 (6½-ounce) package corn muffin mix
⅓ cup milk
1 egg
½ cup shredded Cheddar cheese (2 ounces)
¼ cup sliced green onions

Cook beef, green peppers, onion and garlic in large skillet over medium-high heat until beef is browned, stirring occasionally to break up beef. Stir in steak sauce, tomatoes, seasoning mix, cumin and pepper flakes. Heat to a boil; reduce heat. Cover; simmer 10 to 15 minutes to blend flavors.

Meanwhile, mix corn muffin mix according to package directions, using milk and egg. Drop batter into 6 mounds on chili mixture. Cover; simmer 10 to 12 minutes. (Do not lift cover.) Sprinkle with cheese and green onions. Serve immediately. *Makes 6 servings*

Nell's Chili con Carne

  2 tablespoons vegetable oil
  2 cups diced onions
  1 green bell pepper, seeded and chopped
  3 cloves garlic, minced
  2 pounds lean, coarsely ground beef
  2 cups dried kidney beans, soaked overnight
  1 jar (32 ounces) NEWMAN'S OWN® Spaghetti Sauce
  2 to 3 cups water
  2 to 3 tablespoons chili powder
  1 teaspoon ground cumin
    Salt and black pepper
  1 cup chopped celery
  1 can (8¾ ounces) whole kernel corn, drained
    Sour cream and lime wedges (optional)

173

Heat oil in Dutch oven over medium-high heat. Add onions, bell pepper and garlic; cook and stir until vegetables are tender. Add beef; cook until browned. Add kidney beans, Newman's Own® Spaghetti Sauce, water, chili powder, cumin, and salt and black pepper to taste. Simmer, uncovered, 1 hour, stirring frequently. Add celery and corn and simmer 1 hour. Garnish with sour cream and lime wedges, if desired. *Makes 8 servings*

Note: Three cups of cooked rice can be substituted for meat to make vegetarian chili.

Texas Chili

4 tablespoons vegetable oil, divided
2 large onions, chopped
3 large cloves garlic, minced
2 pounds boneless sirloin or round steak, cut into ½-inch cubes
1 pound ground beef
2 cans (16 ounces each) tomatoes in purée
1 can (15 to 19 ounces) red kidney beans, undrained
⅓ cup *Frank's® RedHot®* Cayenne Pepper Sauce
¼ cup chili powder
2 tablespoons ground cumin
1 tablespoon dried oregano leaves
½ teaspoon ground black pepper

1. Heat 1 tablespoon oil in 5-quart saucepan or Dutch oven. Add onions and garlic; cook 5 minutes or until tender. Transfer to small bowl; set aside.

2. Heat remaining 3 tablespoons oil in saucepan. Add sirloin and ground beef in batches; cook about 15 minutes or until well browned. Drain off fat.

3. Stir in remaining ingredients. Bring to a boil over medium-high heat. Return onions and garlic to saucepan. Simmer, partially covered, 1 hour or until meat is tender. Garnish with shredded Cheddar cheese and chopped green onion, if desired.   *Makes 10 servings*

Prep Time: 15 minutes
Cook Time: 1 hour 20 minutes

174

Texas Chili

Texas-Style Chili

Nonstick cooking spray
1 pound lean boneless beef chuck, cut into ½-inch pieces
2 cups chopped onions
5 cloves garlic, minced
2 tablespoons chili powder
1 tablespoon ground cumin
1 teaspoon ground coriander
1 teaspoon dried oregano leaves
2½ cups reduced-sodium beef broth
1 cup prepared salsa or picante sauce
2 cans (16 ounces each) pinto or red beans (or one can of each), rinsed and drained
½ cup chopped fresh cilantro
½ cup nonfat sour cream
1 cup chopped ripe tomatoes

176

1. Spray Dutch oven or large saucepan with cooking spray; heat over medium-high heat until hot. Add beef, onions and garlic; cook and stir until beef is no longer pink, about 5 minutes. Sprinkle mixture with chili powder, cumin, coriander and oregano; mix well. Add beef broth and salsa; bring to a boil. Cover; simmer 45 minutes.

2. Stir in beans; continue to simmer uncovered 30 minutes or until beef is tender and chili has thickened, stirring occasionally.

3. Stir in cilantro. Ladle into bowls; top with sour cream and tomatoes. Garnish with pickled jalapeño peppers, if desired.

Makes 8 servings

Texas-Style Chili

Winter White Chili

½ pound boneless pork loin *or* 2 boneless pork chops, cut into ½-inch cubes
½ cup chopped onion
1 teaspoon vegetable oil
1 (16-ounce) can navy beans, drained
1 (16-ounce) can chick-peas, drained
1 (16-ounce) can white kernel corn, drained
1 (14½-ounce) can chicken broth
1 cup cooked wild rice
1 (4-ounce) can diced green chilies, drained
1½ teaspoons ground cumin
¼ teaspoon garlic powder
⅛ teaspoon hot pepper sauce
   Chopped parsley and shredded cheese

In 4-quart saucepan, sauté pork and onion in oil over medium-high heat until onion is soft and pork is lightly browned, about 5 minutes. Stir in remaining ingredients except parsley and cheese. Cover and simmer for 20 minutes. Serve each portion garnished with parsley and shredded cheese.   *Makes 6 servings*

Preparation Time: 10 minutes
Cooking Time: 25 minutes

*Favorite recipe from **National Pork Board***

Chilly Day Chili

2 medium onions, chopped
1 green pepper, chopped
2 tablespoons vegetable oil
2 pounds lean ground beef
2 to 3 tablespoons chili powder
1 can (14½ ounces) tomatoes, cut into bite-size pieces
1 can (15 ounces) tomato sauce
½ cup HEINZ® Tomato Ketchup
1 teaspoon salt
¼ teaspoon black pepper
2 cans (15½ ounces each) red kidney beans, partially drained

In large saucepan or Dutch oven, cook and stir onions and green pepper in oil until tender. Add beef; cook until beef is no longer pink, stirring occasionally. Drain excess fat. Stir in chili powder, then add tomatoes, tomato sauce, ketchup, salt and pepper. Simmer, uncovered, 30 minutes, stirring occasionally. Add kidney beans; simmer for an additional 15 minutes.

Makes 8 servings (about 8 cups)

179

Texas Ranch Chili Beans

1 pound lean ground beef
1 can (28 ounces) whole peeled tomatoes, undrained
2 cans (15½ ounces each) chili beans
1 cup chopped onions
1 cup water
1 packet (1 ounce) HIDDEN VALLEY® The Original Ranch® Salad Dressing & Seasoning Mix
1 teaspoon chili powder
1 bay leaf

In Dutch oven, brown beef over medium-high heat; drain off fat. Add tomatoes, breaking up with spoon. Stir in beans, onions, water, salad dressing mix, chili powder and bay leaf. Bring to boil; reduce heat and simmer, uncovered, 1 hour, stirring occasionally. Remove bay leaf just before serving.

Makes 8 servings

Three-Bean Caribbean Chili

1 tablespoon olive oil
1 large onion, chopped
2 cloves garlic, minced
1 jalapeño pepper,* seeded and minced
2 large red or green bell peppers, diced
1 tablespoon plus 2 teaspoons sweet paprika
1 tablespoon plus 2 teaspoons chili powder
2 teaspoons ground cumin
2 teaspoons sugar
½ teaspoon salt
¼ teaspoon ground cloves
1 can (6 ounces) tomato paste
3 cups water
1 can (15 ounces) red kidney beans, drained
1 can (15 ounces) cannellini beans, drained
1 can (15 ounces) black beans, drained
1 tablespoon balsamic vinegar
    Mango Salsa (recipe page 322)
    Hot cooked brown rice

*Jalapeño peppers can sting and irritate the skin; wear rubber gloves when handling peppers and do not touch eyes. Wash hands after handling peppers.

1. Heat oil in large saucepan over medium heat until hot. Add onion and garlic; cook and stir 4 minutes. Add jalapeño and bell peppers; cook and stir 5 minutes or until tender.

2. Add paprika, chili powder, cumin, sugar, salt and cloves; cook and stir 1 minute.

3. Stir in tomato paste and water until blended. Bring to a boil over high heat. Reduce heat to low. Cover and simmer 15 minutes. Stir in beans and vinegar; partially cover and simmer 15 minutes or until hot.

4. Meanwhile, prepare Mango Salsa.

5. Serve chili over rice. Top with Mango Salsa. Garnish, if desired.

Makes 6 (1-cup) servings
continued on page 182

Three-Bean Caribbean Chili

Three-Bean Caribbean Chili, continued

Mango Salsa

1 large mango, peeled and cut into ¾-inch cubes
1 small, firm, ripe banana, peeled and cubed
3 tablespoons minced fresh cilantro
1 tablespoon thawed frozen orange juice concentrate
1 teaspoon balsamic vinegar

Combine mango, banana and cilantro in medium bowl. Stir together juice concentrate and vinegar. Pour over fruit; toss.   *Makes 1¼ cups*

Black Bean Vegetarian Chili

1 tablespoon olive oil
2 onions, finely chopped
1 green bell pepper, diced
1 teaspoon ground cumin
1 teaspoon minced garlic
1 to 2 canned chipotle peppers, stemmed and diced, seeds included*
4 cans (15 ounces each) black beans, rinsed and drained
1 can (15 ounces) corn kernels, drained
1 can (15 ounces) diced tomatoes, undrained
1 can (6 ounces) tomato paste plus 3 cans water
½ teaspoon salt
½ teaspoon black pepper
   Sour cream
   Whole wheat flour tortillas (optional)

*Chipotle peppers come in 7-ounce cans packed in adobo sauce. Unused peppers and sauce may be frozen in small plastic bags for later use. Use 1 pepper for mildly spicy chili and 2 peppers for very spicy chili.

1. Heat olive oil in Dutch oven until hot. Reserve ½ cup chopped onions. Add remaining onions and bell pepper to Dutch oven; cook and stir 5 minutes or until soft. Add cumin; cook and stir about 10 seconds. Add garlic; cook and stir 1 minute.

2. Stir in chipotle peppers, black beans, corn, tomatoes with juice, tomato paste, water, salt and black pepper. Bring to a boil. Reduce heat and simmer 30 minutes.

3. Serve with sour cream, reserved onions and whole wheat flour tortillas, if desired.

Makes 8 servings

Rice and Chick-Pea Chili

⅔ cup **UNCLE BEN'S® ORIGINAL CONVERTED® Brand Rice**
1 can (15 ounces) chick-peas, undrained
1 can (15 ounces) diced tomatoes, undrained
1 can (8 ounces) diced green chilies
1 cup frozen corn
¼ **cup chopped fresh cilantro**
1 tablespoon taco seasoning
½ **cup (2 ounces) shredded reduced-fat Cheddar cheese**

1. In medium saucepan, bring 1¾ cups water and rice to a boil. Cover, reduce heat and simmer 15 minutes.

2. Add remaining ingredients except cheese. Cook over low heat 10 minutes. Serve in bowls sprinkled with cheese.

Makes 4 servings

Helpful Hint

To round out the meal, serve this hearty vegetarian chili with fruit and corn bread fresh from the oven.

183

Chili with Beans and Corn

1 (16-ounce) can black-eyed peas or cannellini beans, rinsed and drained
1 (16-ounce) can kidney or navy beans, rinsed and drained
1 (15-ounce) can whole tomatoes, chopped and drained
1 onion, chopped
1 cup canned or frozen corn
1 cup water
½ cup chopped green onions
½ cup tomato paste
¼ cup diced jalapeño peppers*
1 tablespoon chili powder
1 teaspoon ground cumin
1 teaspoon prepared mustard
½ teaspoon dried oregano leaves

*Jalapeño peppers can sting and irritate the skin; wear rubber gloves when handling peppers and do not touch eyes. Wash hands after handling peppers.

184

SLOW COOKER DIRECTIONS
Combine all ingredients in slow cooker. Cover and cook on LOW 8 to 10 hours or on HIGH 4 to 5 hours.

Makes 6 to 8 servings

This vegetarian chili is easy to assemble. Simply combine all ingredients in a slow cooker in the morning and the chili will be ready for dinner eight hours later. Complete the meal with hot bread and a simple dessert.

Chili with Beans and Corn

CONTENTS

Fiery Chile Beef, page 188

Shredded Apricot Pork
Sandwiches, page 254

Mexicali Chicken,
page 290

Cook-Ahead Beef Meals

Meatballs in Burgundy Sauce

   60 frozen fully-cooked meatballs
    3 cups chopped onions
 1½ cups water
    1 cup red wine
    2 packages (about 8 ounces) beef gravy mix
   ¼ cup ketchup
    1 tablespoon dried oregano leaves
     Hot cooked noodles

1. Combine all ingredients except noodles in slow cooker; stir to blend. Cover; cook on HIGH 5 hours.

2. Serve with noodles.   *Makes 6 to 8 servings*

Serving Suggestion: Serve as an appetizer with cocktail picks and remaining sauce as a dip.

Meatballs in Burgundy Sauce

Fiery Chile Beef

1 flank steak (about 1 to 1½ pounds)
1 can (28 ounces) diced tomatoes, undrained
1 can (15 ounces) pinto beans, rinsed and drained
1 medium onion, chopped
2 cloves garlic, minced
½ teaspoon salt
½ teaspoon ground cumin
¼ teaspoon black pepper
1 canned chipotle chile pepper in adobo sauce
1 teaspoon adobo sauce from canned chile pepper
Flour tortillas

1. Cut flank steak into 6 evenly-sized pieces. Place flank steak, tomatoes with juice, beans, onion, garlic, salt, cumin and black pepper into slow cooker.

2. Dice chile pepper. Add pepper and adobo sauce to slow cooker; mix well. Cover; cook on LOW 7 to 8 hours. Serve with tortillas.   *Makes 6 servings*

Note: Chipotle chile peppers are dried, smoked jalapeño peppers with a very hot yet smoky and sweet flavor. They can be found dried, pickled and canned in adobo sauce.

Slow Cooker Round Steak with Gravy

1 pound beef round steak
1 can (10¾ ounces) condensed cream of chicken or cream of mushroom soup
½ cup water
1 package (1 ounce) dry onion soup mix

Combine all ingredients in slow cooker. Cover; cook on LOW 8 hours or on HIGH 6 hours.

Makes 4 servings

Fiery Chile Beef

Picadillo

1 pound ground beef
1 small onion, chopped
1 clove garlic, minced
1 can (14½ ounces) diced tomatoes, undrained
¼ cup golden raisins
1 tablespoon chili powder
1 tablespoon cider vinegar
½ teaspoon ground cumin
½ teaspoon dried oregano leaves
½ teaspoon ground cinnamon
¼ teaspoon red pepper flakes
1 teaspoon salt
¼ cup slivered almonds (optional)

1. Cook ground beef, onion and garlic in large nonstick skillet over medium heat until beef is no longer pink; drain. Place mixture into slow cooker.

2. Add tomatoes, raisins, chili powder, vinegar, cumin, oregano, cinnamon and pepper flakes to slow cooker. Cover; cook on LOW 6 to 7 hours. Stir in salt. Garnish with almonds, if desired.

Makes 4 servings

SLOW COOKING SECRET

Browning meats before adding to the slow cooker helps reduce the fat. Just remember to drain off the fat in the skillet before transferring meat to the slow cooker.

Braciola

1 can (28 ounces) tomato sauce
2½ teaspoons dried oregano leaves, divided
1¼ teaspoons dried basil leaves, divided
1 teaspoon salt
½ pound bulk hot Italian sausage
½ cup chopped onion
¼ cup grated Parmesan cheese
2 cloves garlic, minced
1 tablespoon dried parsley flakes
2½ pounds flank steak

1. Combine tomato sauce, 2 teaspoons oregano, 1 teaspoon basil and salt in medium bowl; set aside.

2. Cook sausage in large nonstick skillet over medium-high heat until no longer pink stirring to separate; drain well. Combine sausage, onion, cheese, garlic, parsley, remaining ½ teaspoon oregano and ¼ teaspoon basil in medium bowl; set aside.

3. Place steak on countertop between two pieces waxed paper. Pound with meat mallet until steak is ⅛ to ¼ inch thick. Cut steak into about 3-inch wide strips.

4. Spoon sausage mixture evenly onto each strip. Roll up jelly-roll style, securing meat with toothpicks. Place each roll in slow cooker. Pour reserved tomato sauce mixture over meat. Cover; cook on LOW 6 to 8 hours.

5. Cut each roll into slices. Arrange slices on dinner plates. Top with hot tomato sauce.

Makes 6 to 8 servings

Spicy Italian Beef

1 boneless beef chuck roast (3 to 4 pounds)
1 jar (12 ounces) pepperoncini (mild salad peppers)
1 can (14½ ounces) beef broth
1 can (12 ounces) beer
1 package (1 ounce) Italian salad dressing mix
1 loaf French bread, thickly sliced
10 slices provolone cheese (optional)

1. Trim visible fat from roast. Cut roast, if necessary, to fit into slow cooker, leaving meat in as many large pieces as possible.

2. Drain peppers; pull off stem ends. Add to slow cooker along with broth, beer and dressing mix; do not stir. Cover; cook on low 8 to 10 hours.

3. Remove meat from sauce; shred with 2 forks. Return shredded meat to slow cooker; mix well.

4. Serve on French bread slice, topped with cheese, if desired. Add sauce and peppers as desired.

Makes 8 to 10 servings

Spicy Italian Beef

Italian-Style Pot Roast

2 teaspoons minced garlic
1 teaspoon salt
1 teaspoon dried basil leaves
1 teaspoon dried oregano leaves
¼ teaspoon red pepper flakes
2½ to 3 pounds beef bottom round rump or chuck shoulder roast
1 large onion, quartered and thinly sliced
1½ cups prepared tomato basil or marinara spaghetti sauce
2 cans (16 ounces each) cannellini or Great Northern beans, drained
¼ cup shredded fresh basil or chopped Italian parsley

1. Combine garlic, salt, basil, oregano and pepper flakes in small bowl; rub over roast.

2. Place ½ onion slices into slow cooker. Cut roast in half to fit into slow cooker. Place one half of roast over onion slices; top with remaining onion slices and other half of roast. Pour spaghetti sauce over roast. Cover; cook on LOW 8 to 9 hours or until roast is fork tender.

3. Remove roast from cooking liquid; tent with foil.

4. Let liquid in slow cooker stand 5 minutes to allow fat to rise. Skim off fat.

5. Stir beans into liquid. Cover; cook on HIGH 10 to 15 minutes or until beans are hot. Carve roast across the grain into thin slices. Serve with bean mixture and garnish with basil.

Makes 6 to 8 servings

Italian-Style Pot Roast

Slow Cooker Steak Fajitas

1 pound beef flank steak, cut across the grain into thin strips
1 medium onion, cut into strips
½ cup medium salsa
2 tablespoons fresh lime juice
2 tablespoons chopped fresh cilantro
2 cloves garlic, minced
1 tablespoon chili powder
1 teaspoon ground cumin
½ teaspoon salt
1 small green bell pepper, cut into strips
1 small red bell pepper, cut into strips
Flour tortillas, warmed
Additional salsa (optional)

1. Combine all ingredients except bell peppers, tortillas and additional salsa in slow cooker. Cover; cook on LOW 5 to 6 hours. Add bell peppers. Cover; cook on LOW 1 hour.

2. Serve with flour tortillas and additional salsa, if desired.   *Makes 4 servings*

Slow Cooker Steak Fajitas

Round Steak

1 round steak (1½ pounds), trimmed and cut into 4 equal-size pieces
¼ cup all-purpose flour
1 teaspoon black pepper
½ teaspoon salt
1 tablespoon vegetable oil
1 can (10¾ ounces) condensed cream of mushroom soup
¾ cup water
1 medium onion, quartered
1 can (4 ounces) sliced mushrooms, drained
¼ cup milk
1 package (1 ounce) dry onion soup mix
   Salt and black pepper
   Ground sage
   Dried thyme leaves
1 bay leaf

1. Place steaks in large plastic bag food storage bag. Close bag and pound with mallet to tenderize. Combine flour, black pepper and salt in small bowl; add to bag with steaks. Shake to coat meat evenly.

2. Heat oil in large nonstick skillet. Remove steaks from bag; shake off excess flour. Add steaks to skillet; brown on both sides.

3. Transfer steaks with pan juices, mushroom soup, water, onion, mushrooms, milk, soup mix seasonings to taste and bay leaf to slow cooker. Cover; cook on LOW 5 to 6 hours or until steaks are tender. Remove bay leaf before serving.   *Makes 4 servings*

Slow-Cooked Smothered Steak

⅓ cup all-purpose flour
1 teaspoon garlic salt
½ teaspoon black pepper
1½ pounds beef chuck or round steak, cut into strips
1 large onion, sliced
1 to 2 medium green bell peppers, cut into strips
1 can (4 ounces) sliced mushrooms, drained
¼ cup teriyaki sauce
1 package (10 ounces) frozen French-style green beans

1. Combine flour, garlic salt and black pepper in medium bowl. Add steak strips, tossing to coat with flour mixture. Place into slow cooker.

2. Layer remaining ingredients in slow cooker. Cover; cook on HIGH 1 hour. Reduce heat to LOW; cook on LOW 8 hours or on HIGH 5 hours.

Makes 6 servings

SLOW COOKING SECRET

Spinning the cover until the condensation falls off allows you to see inside the slow cooker without removing the lid, which delays the cooking time.

Mama Mia Spaghetti Sauce

1 tablespoon olive oil
1 package (8 ounces) sliced mushrooms
½ cup finely chopped carrots
1 clove garlic, minced
1 shallot, minced
1 pound lean ground beef
2 cups canned or fresh crushed tomatoes
½ cup dry red wine or beef broth
2 tablespoons tomato paste
1 teaspoon salt
1 teaspoon dried oregano leaves
½ teaspoon dried basil leaves
¼ teaspoon black pepper
4 cups cooked spaghetti
Grated Parmesan cheese (optional)

1. Heat oil in large skillet over medium-high heat until hot. Add mushrooms, carrots, garlic and shallot to skillet. Cook and stir 5 minutes. Place vegetables in slow cooker.

2. Add ground beef to skillet; brown, stirring to break up meat. Drain fat. Place beef into slow cooker.

3. Add tomatoes, wine, tomato paste, salt, oregano, basil and pepper. Cover; cook on HIGH 3 to 4 hours. Serve sauce with cooked spaghetti. Sprinkle with Parmesan cheese, if desired.

Makes 5 servings

Smothered Beef Patties

Worcestershire sauce
Garlic powder
Salt
Black pepper
1 can (14½ ounces) Mexican-style diced tomatoes with chilies, undrained, divided
8 frozen beef patties, unthawed
1 onion, cut into 8 slices

Sprinkle bottom of slow cooker with small amount of Worcestershire sauce, garlic powder, salt, pepper and 2 tablespoons tomatoes. Place 1 frozen beef patty on seasonings. Season top of patty with more of same seasonings. Place slice of onion on top each patty. Repeat layers. Cover; cook on LOW 8 hours. *Makes 8 servings*

Serving Suggestion: Serve with mashed potatoes and Caesar salad. Also delicious with steamed rice.

Easy Beef Stew

1½ to 2 pounds beef for stew
4 medium potatoes, cubed
4 carrots, cut into 1½-inch pieces *or* 4 cups baby carrots
1 medium onion, cut into 8 wedges
2 cans (8 ounces each) tomato sauce
1 teaspoon salt
½ teaspoon black pepper

Combine all ingredients in slow cooker. Cover; cook on LOW 8 to 10 hours or until vegetables are tender. *Makes 6 to 8 servings*

Smothered Beef Patty

Slow-Cooked Korean Beef Short Ribs

  4 to 4½ pounds beef short ribs
  ¼ cup chopped green onions with tops
  ¼ cup tamari or soy sauce
  ¼ cup beef broth or water
  1 tablespoon brown sugar
  2 teaspoons minced fresh ginger
  2 teaspoons minced garlic
  ½ teaspoon black pepper
  2 teaspoons Asian sesame oil
    Hot cooked rice or linguini pasta
  2 teaspoons sesame seeds, toasted

1. Place ribs in slow cooker. Combine green onions, soy sauce, broth, brown sugar, ginger, garlic and pepper in medium bowl; mix well and pour over ribs. Cover; cook on LOW 7 to 8 hours or until ribs are fork tender.

2. Remove ribs from cooking liquid, cool slightly. Trim excess fat. Cut rib meat into bite-sized pieces discarding bones and fat.

3. Let cooking liquid stand 5 minutes to allow fat to rise. Skim off fat.

4. Stir sesame oil into liquid. Return beef to slow cooker. Cover; cook on LOW 15 to 30 minutes or until mixture is hot. Serve with rice or pasta; garnish with sesame seeds.

Makes 6 servings

Variation: 3 pounds boneless short ribs may be substituted for beef short ribs.

Beef with Green Chilies

¼ cup plus 1 tablespoon all-purpose flour
½ teaspoon salt
¼ teaspoon black pepper
1 pound beef for stew
1 tablespoon vegetable oil
2 cloves garlic, minced
1 cup beef broth
1 can (7 ounces) diced mild green chilies, drained
½ teaspoon dried oregano leaves
2 tablespoons water
Hot cooked rice (optional)
Diced tomato (optional)

1. Combine ¼ cup flour, salt and pepper in resealable plastic food storage bag. Add beef; shake to coat beef. Heat oil in large skillet over medium-high heat. Add beef and garlic. Brown beef on all sides. Place beef mixture into slow cooker. Add broth to skillet scraping up any browned bits. Pour broth mixture into slow cooker. Add chilies and oregano.

2. Cover; cook on LOW 7 to 8 hours. For thicker sauce, combine remaining 1 tablespoon flour and water in small bowl stirring until mixture is smooth. Stir mixture into slow cooker; mix well. Cover and cook until thickened.

3. Serve with rice and garnish with diced tomato, if desired.   *Makes 4 servings*

Variation: Use two cans of chilies for a slightly hotter taste.

Peppered Beef Tips

1 pound beef sirloin tips
2 cloves garlic, minced
Black pepper
1 can (10¾ ounces) condensed French onion soup
1 can (10¾ ounces) condensed cream of mushroom soup

Place beef tips in slow cooker. Sprinkle with garlic and pepper. Pour soups over beef. Cover; cook on LOW 8 to 10 hours. *Makes 2 to 3 servings*

Serving Suggestion: Serve over cooked noodles or rice.

Beef with Mushroom and Red Wine Gravy

1½ pounds well-trimmed beef stew meat, cut into 1-inch cubes
2 medium onions, cut into ½-inch wedges
1 package (8 ounces) sliced baby button, cremini or other fresh mushrooms
1 package (about 1 ounce) dry beefy onion soup mix
3 tablespoons cornstarch
⅛ teaspoon salt
⅛ teaspoon black pepper
1½ cups dry red wine

Place beef, onions and mushrooms into slow cooker. Sprinkle with soup mix, cornstarch, salt and pepper. Pour wine over all. Cover; cook on LOW 10 to 12 hours or on HIGH 5 to 6 hours. *Makes 6 servings*

Peppered Beef Tips

Autumn Delight

4 to 6 beef cubed steaks
Olive oil
2 to 3 cans (10¾ ounces each) condensed cream of mushroom soup
1 to 1½ cups water
1 package (1 ounce) dry onion or mushroom soup mix

1. Lightly brown cubed steaks in oil in large nonstick skillet over medium heat.

2. Place steaks into slow cooker. Add soup, water (½ cup water per can of soup) and soup mix; stir. Cover; cook on LOW 4 to 6 hours.   *Makes 4 to 6 servings*

Best Ever Slow Cooker Pot Roast

1 beef chuck shoulder roast (3 to 4 pounds)
1 can (10 ounces) beef gravy
½ cup dry red wine
1 package (1 ounce) au jus mix
½ package Italian salad dressing mix
2 tablespoons all-purpose flour
½ cup cold water

1. Place roast in slow cooker. Combine gravy, wine, au jus mix and salad dressing mix into medium bowl. Pour mixture over meat. Cover; cook on LOW 8 to 10 hours.

2. Remove roast to plate; cover with foil to keep warm. Turn slow cooker to HIGH. Mix flour into water until smooth. Stir into juices in slow cooker. Cook 15 minutes or until thickened.

Makes 8 servings

Autumn Delight

Slow-Cooked Pot Roast

1 tablespoon vegetable oil
1 beef brisket (3 to 4 pounds)
1 tablespoon garlic powder, divided
1 tablespoon salt, divided
1 tablespoon black pepper, divided
1 teaspoon paprika, divided
5 to 6 new potatoes, cut into quarters
4 to 5 medium onions, sliced
1 pound baby carrots
1 can (14½ ounces) beef broth

1. Heat 1 tablespoon oil on HIGH in slow cooker. Brown brisket on all sides. Remove brisket to plate. Season with 1½ teaspoons garlic powder, 1½ teaspoons salt, 1½ teaspoons pepper and ½ teaspoon paprika; set aside.

2. Season potatoes with remaining 1½ teaspoons garlic powder, 1½ teaspoons salt, 1½ teaspoons pepper and ½ teaspoon paprika. Add potatoes and onions to slow cooker. Cook on HIGH, stirring occasionally, until browned.

3. Return brisket to slow cooker. Add carrots and broth. Cover; cook on HIGH 4 to 5 hours or on LOW 8 to 10 hours or until meat is tender. *Makes 6 to 8 servings*

Serving Suggestion: Arrange potatoes and carrots around the sliced beef. Spoon on broth to keep the meat moist.

Harvest Beef Stew

1 tablespoon olive oil
1½ pounds beef for stew
1 can (28 ounces) stewed tomatoes, undrained
6 carrots, cut into 1-inch pieces
3 medium potatoes, cut into 1-inch pieces
3 ribs celery, chopped (about 1 cup)
1 medium onion, sliced
1 cup apple juice
2 tablespoons dried parsley flakes
1 tablespoon dried basil leaves
2 teaspoons salt
1 clove garlic, minced
½ teaspoon black pepper
2 bay leaves
¼ cup all-purpose flour (optional)
½ cup warm water (optional)

1. Heat oil in large skillet over medium-low heat. Brown stew meat on all sides. Drain excess fat.

2. Place browned meat and all remaining ingredients except flour and water into slow cooker. Mix well. Cover; cook on HIGH 6 to 7 hours.

3. Before serving, thicken gravy, if desired. Combine flour and warm water in small bowl, stirring well until all lumps are gone. Add mixture to liquid in slow cooker; mix well. Cook 10 to 20 minutes or until sauce thickens. Remove and discard bay leaves before serving.

Makes 6 servings

Beef and Vegetables in Rich Burgundy Sauce

1 package (8 ounces) sliced mushrooms
1 package (8 ounces) baby carrots
1 medium green bell pepper, cut into thin strips
1 boneless beef chuck roast (2½ pounds)
1 can (10½ ounces) condensed golden mushroom soup
¼ cup dry red wine or beef broth
1 tablespoon Worcestershire sauce
1 package (1 ounce) dry onion soup mix
¼ teaspoon black pepper
3 tablespoons cornstarch
2 tablespoons water
4 cups hot cooked noodles
   Chopped fresh parsley (optional)

1. Place mushrooms, carrots and bell pepper in slow cooker. Place roast on top of vegetables. Combine mushroom soup, wine, Worcestershire sauce, soup mix and black pepper in medium bowl; mix well. Pour soup mixture over roast. Cover; cook on LOW 8 to 10 hours.

2. Transfer roast to cutting board; cover with foil. Let stand 10 to 15 minutes before slicing.

3. Blend cornstarch and water until smooth. Turn slow cooker to HIGH. Stir cornstarch mixture into vegetable mixture; cook 10 minutes or until thickened. Serve beef and vegetables with sauce over cooked noodles. Garnish with parsley, if desired. *Makes 6 to 8 servings*

Beef and Vegetables in Rich Burgundy Sauce

Saucy Braised Beef

2 pounds beef top round, trimmed and cut into bite-size pieces
1 tablespoon mixed dried herbs
  Salt
  Black pepper
2 tablespoons oil
2 cups baby carrots
1 large yellow onion, thinly sliced
1 medium zucchini, cut into 1-inch slices
2 tablespoons minced garlic
1 teaspoon dried oregano leaves
1 can (8 ounces) tomato sauce
1 can (6 ounces) tomato paste
½ cup molasses
2 tablespoons red wine vinegar
2 teaspoons hot pepper sauce

1. Lightly season beef with mixed herbs, salt and pepper to taste. Heat oil in Dutch oven or large skillet over medium-low heat. Brown meat on all sides. Drain excess fat. Place beef into slow cooker.

2. Add carrots, onion, zucchini, garlic and oregano to Dutch oven. Cook over medium-low heat 4 to 5 minutes or until onion is tender, stirring occasionally. Add vegetable mixture and remaining ingredients to slow cooker; mix well.

3. Cover; cook on LOW 8 to 10 hours. *Makes 4 to 6 servings*

Beef with Apples and Sweet Potatoes

2 pounds boneless beef chuck shoulder roast
1 can (40 ounces) sweet potatoes, drained
2 small onions, sliced
2 apples, cored and sliced
½ cup beef broth
2 cloves garlic, minced
1 teaspoon salt
1 teaspoon dried thyme leaves, divided
¾ teaspoon black pepper, divided
1 tablespoon cornstarch
¼ teaspoon ground cinnamon
2 tablespoons cold water

1. Trim fat from beef and cut into 2-inch pieces. Place beef, sweet potatoes, onions, apples, beef broth, garlic, salt, ½ teaspoon thyme and ½ teaspoon pepper in slow cooker. Cover; cook on LOW 8 to 9 hours.

2. Transfer beef, sweet potatoes and apples to platter; keep warm. Let liquid stand 5 minutes to allow fat to rise. Skim off fat.

3. Combine cornstarch, remaining ½ teaspoon thyme, ¼ teaspoon pepper, cinnamon and water; stir into cooking liquid. Cook 15 minutes or until juices are thickened. Serve sauce with beef, sweet potatoes and apples. *Makes 6 servings*

Beef Roll Ups

1 beef round steak (1½ pounds), ½ inch thick
4 slices bacon
½ cup diced green bell pepper
¼ cup diced onion
¼ cup diced celery
1 can (10 ounces) beef gravy

1. Cut steak into 4 pieces. Place 1 bacon slice on each piece.

2. Combine bell pepper, onion, and celery in medium bowl. Place about ¼ cup mixture on each piece of meat. Roll up meat jelly-roll style; secure with wooden toothpicks.

3. Place beef rolls in slow cooker. Pour gravy evenly over steaks. Cover; cook on LOW 8 to 10 hours. Skim off fat before serving. *Makes 4 servings*

Serving Suggestion: Serve with mashed potatoes or over rice.

Easy Beef Burgundy

1½ pounds beef round steak, cut into 1-inch pieces or beef for stew
1 can (10¾ ounces) condensed cream of mushroom soup
1 cup red wine
1 small onion, chopped
1 can (4 ounces) sliced mushrooms, drained
1 package (1 ounce) dry onion soup mix
1 tablespoon minced garlic

Combine all ingredients in slow cooker. Cover; cook on LOW 6 to 8 hours or until beef is tender. *Makes 4 to 6 servings*

Serving Suggestion: Serve over noodles, rice or mashed potatoes.

Beef Roll Up

Corned Beef and Cabbage

1 head cabbage (1½ pounds), cut into 6 wedges
4 ounces baby carrots
1 corned beef (3 pounds) with seasoning packet*
1 quart (4 cups) water
⅓ cup prepared mustard (optional)
⅓ cup honey (optional)

If seasoning packet is not perforated, poke several small holes with tip of paring knife.

1. Place cabbage in slow cooker; top with carrots.

2. Place seasoning packet on top of vegetables. Place corned beef, fat side up, over seasoning packet and vegetables. Add water. Cover; cook on LOW 10 hours.

3. Discard seasoning packet. Just before serving, combine mustard and honey in small bowl. Use as dipping sauce, if desired.   *Makes 6 servings*

Beef Stew

1 pound potatoes, cut into 1-inch cubes
1 pound baby carrots
1 large onion, chopped *or* 1 package (10 ounces) frozen peas and pearl onions
2 pounds beef for stew
1 can (10¾ ounces) condensed cream of mushroom soup
1 can (10¾ ounces) condensed French onion soup

Place potatoes in bottom of slow cooker; top with baby carrots and onion. Place meat on top. Pour soups over top. Cover; cook on LOW 8 to 10 hours.   *Makes 8 servings*

Corned Beef and Cabbage

Beef and Noodles

  1 tablespoon vegetable oil
  1 beef chuck shoulder roast (3 pounds)
  1 can (10¾ ounces) condensed cream of mushroom or cream of potato soup
  1 cup cooking sherry
  1 cup water
  1 package (1 ounce) dry onion soup mix
  1 package (12 ounces) egg noodles, cooked according to package directions

1. Heat oil in large skillet over medium-low heat. Brown roast on all sides. Drain excess fat.

2. Place meat and remaining ingredients except noodles into slow cooker. Cover; cook on LOW 8 hours, stirring once or twice during cooking.

3. Serve roast over noodles.   *Makes 8 servings*

So Simple Supper!

  1 beef chuck shoulder roast (3 to 4 pounds)
  1 package (1 ounce) mushroom gravy mix
  1 package (1 ounce) dry onion gravy mix
  1 package (1 ounce) au jus gravy mix
  3 cups water
     Assorted vegetables (potatoes, carrots, onions, celery, etc.)

1. Place roast in slow cooker. Combine gravy mixes and water in large bowl . Pour gravy mixture over roast. Cover; cook on LOW 4 hours.

2. Add vegetables and cook 2 more hours or until meat and vegetables are tender.

                                                                      Makes 8 servings

Ranch Stew

- 2 pounds beef for stew
- 6 medium potatoes, diced
- 2 cups sliced carrots
- 2 medium onions, chopped
- 1 medium green bell pepper, chopped (optional)
- 1 cup diced celery (optional)
- 1 can (10¾ ounces) condensed tomato soup
- 1 soup can water
- 2 tablespoons tapioca
- 1 tablespoon Worcestershire sauce
- 2 teaspoons salt
- 1 teaspoon soy sauce
- ¼ teaspoon black pepper
- 1 bay leaf

Combine all ingredients in slow cooker. Cover; cook on LOW 10 to 12 hours or until tender. Remove and discard bay leaf before serving.

Makes 6 servings

SLOW COOKING SECRET

Vegetables such as potatoes and carrots can sometimes take longer to cook in a slow cooker than the meat. Place evenly cut vegetables on the bottom or along the sides of the slow cooker when possible.

Slow Cooker Stuffed Peppers

1 package (7 ounces) Spanish rice mix
1 pound ground beef
½ cup diced celery
1 small onion, chopped
1 egg
4 medium green bell peppers, halved lengthwise, cored and seeded
1 can (28 ounces) whole peeled tomatoes, undrained
1 can (10¾ ounces) condensed tomato soup
1 cup water

1. Set aside seasoning packet from rice. Combine beef, rice mix, celery, onion and egg in large bowl. Divide meat mixture evenly among pepper halves.

2. Pour tomatoes with juice into slow cooker. Arrange filled pepper halves on top of tomatoes. Combine tomato soup, water and reserved rice mix seasoning packet in large bowl. Pour over peppers. Cover; cook on LOW 8 to 10 hours. *Makes 4 servings*

Slow Cooker Beef & Noodles

1 can (10½ ounces) condensed French onion soup
1 can (10¾ ounces) condensed cream of mushroom soup
1 to 1½ pounds beef for stew
1 bag (12 ounces) extra-wide egg noodles, cooked

1. Combine soups and meat in slow cooker; stir. Cover; cook on LOW 8 to 10 hours.

2. Serve with prepared noodles. *Makes 4 to 6 servings*

Slow Cooker Stuffed Peppers

Country-Style Steak

4 to 6 beef cubed steaks
All-purpose flour
1 tablespoon vegetable oil
1 package (1 ounce) dry onion soup mix
1 package (1 ounce) brown gravy mix
Water

1. Dust steaks with flour. Heat oil in large skillet over medium-low heat. Brown steaks on both sides. Drain excess fat.

2. Place steaks in slow cooker. Add soup and gravy mixes and enough water to cover meat. Cover; cook on LOW 6 to 8 hours.

Makes 4 to 6 servings

Serving Suggestion: Serve with mashed potatoes.

Slow Cooker Beef Stroganoff

1½ to 2 pounds beef for stew
1 can (10¾ ounces) condensed cream of mushroom soup
1 can (4 ounces) sliced mushrooms, drained
1 package (1 ounce) dry onion soup mix

Combine meat, mushroom soup, mushrooms and onion soup mix in slow cooker. Cover; cook on LOW 6 to 8 hours.

Makes 4 to 6 servings

Serving Suggestion: Serve with hot cooked rice or noodles.

Spaghetti Sauce

- 1 tablespoon olive oil
- 1½ pounds ground beef
- 1 medium onion, chopped
- 1 medium green bell pepper, diced
- 2 cans (28 ounces each) crushed tomatoes, undrained
- 1 can (15 ounces) beef broth
- 1 can (8 ounces) tomato sauce
- 1 can (6 ounces) tomato paste (or more to taste)
- ½ cup grated Parmesan cheese
- 1 tablespoon brown sugar
- 2 teaspoons garlic powder
- 1 teaspoon dried oregano leaves
- 1 teaspoon dried basil leaves

1. Heat oil in large skillet over medium-low heat. Add ground beef, onion and bell pepper. Cook, stirring frequently, until meat is no longer pink and onion is tender. Drain excess fat.

2. Place meat mixture into slow cooker. Add remaining ingredients; stir thoroughly. Cover; cook on LOW 6 to 8 hours.

Makes 6 servings

SLOW COOKING SECRET

Jazz up the flavor of slow cooker dishes by adding a small amount of snipped fresh herbs or freshly ground pepper just before serving.

Mushroom-Beef Stew

1 pound beef stew meat
1 can (10¾ ounces) condensed cream of mushroom soup
2 cans (4 ounces each) sliced mushrooms, drained
1 package (1 ounce) dry onion soup mix

Combine all ingredients in slow cooker. Cover; cook on low 8 to 10 hours.   *Makes 4 servings*

Serving Suggestion: Serve over hot cooked rice or noodles.

Slow Cooker Bean Dish

1 pound extra-lean ground beef
½ pound bacon, cut into 1-inch pieces
1 can (15 ounces) butter beans, drained
1 can (15 ounces) garbanzo beans, drained
1 can (15 ounces) red kidney beans, drained
1 can (15 ounces) pork and beans
1 cup brown sugar
1 cup ketchup
½ cup diced onion
2 tablespoons vinegar

1. Cook and stir ground beef in large skillet over medium-high heat until no longer pink. Drain excess fat.

2. Combine beef and remaining ingredients in slow cooker. Cover; cook on LOW 6 hours.

Makes 8 servings

Mushroom-Beef Stew

Beef Stew with Molasses and Raisins

⅓ cup all-purpose flour
2 teaspoons salt, divided
1½ teaspoons black pepper, divided
2 pounds boneless beef chuck roast, cut into 1½-inch pieces
5 tablespoons oil, divided
2 medium onions, sliced
1 can (28 ounces) diced tomatoes, drained
1 cup beef broth
3 tablespoons molasses
2 tablespoons cider vinegar
4 cloves garlic, minced
2 teaspoons dried thyme leaves
1 teaspoon celery salt
1 bay leaf
8 ounces baby carrots, cut in half lengthwise
2 parsnips, diced
½ cup golden raisins
Salt and black pepper

1. Combine flour, 1½ teaspoons salt and 1 teaspoon pepper in large bowl. Toss meat in flour mixture. Heat 2 tablespoons oil in large skillet or Dutch oven over medium-high heat. Add half of beef and brown on all sides. Set aside browned beef and repeat with 2 tablespoons oil and remaining beef.

2. Add remaining 1 tablespoon oil to skillet. Add onions and cook, stirring to loosen any browned bits, about 5 minutes. Add tomatoes, broth, molasses, vinegar, garlic, thyme, celery salt, bay leaf and remaining ½ teaspoon salt and ½ teaspoon pepper. Bring to a boil. Add browned beef and boil 1 minute.

3. Transfer mixture to slow cooker. Cover; cook on LOW 5 hours or on HIGH 2½ hours. Add carrots, parsnips and raisins. Continue to cook on LOW 1 to 2 hours more or until vegetables are tender. Season to taste with salt and pepper. *Makes 6 to 8 servings*

Beef Stew with Molasses and Raisins

Pot Roast

1 tablespoon vegetable oil
1 beef chuck shoulder roast (3 to 4 pounds)
6 medium potatoes, halved
2 medium onions, quartered
6 carrots, sliced
2 ribs celery, sliced
1 can (14½ ounces) diced tomatoes, undrained (optional)
Salt
Black pepper
Dried oregano leaves
Water
1½ to 2 tablespoons all-purpose flour

1. Heat oil in large skillet over medium-low heat. Add roast; brown on all sides. Drain excess fat.

2. Place roast in slow cooker. Add potatoes, onions, carrots, celery and tomatoes with juice. Season with salt, pepper and oregano to taste. Add enough water to cover bottom of slow cooker by about ½ inch. Cover; cook on LOW 8 to 10 hours.

3. Serve with cooked juices from slow cooker. To make gravy, combine juices with flour in small saucepan. Cook and stir over medium heat until thickened. *Makes 6 to 8 servings*

Barbecue Beef Cubes

 1 boneless beef roast (4 pounds), cut into cubes
 1 can (28 ounces) tomatoes, undrained
 1 can (4 ounces) tomato paste
 1 large onion, chopped
 ¼ cup firmly packed brown sugar
 ¼ cup vinegar
 2 teaspoons salt
 2 teaspoons barbecue spice mix
 2 teaspoons Worcestershire sauce
 2 cloves garlic, minced
 1 teaspoon dry mustard
 ¼ teaspoon black pepper

Place beef cubes in slow cooker. Combine remaining ingredients in large bowl; pour over meat. Cover; cook on LOW 6 to 8 hours or until tender. *Makes 8 servings*

Serving Suggestion: Serve over rice or noodles.

SLOW COOKING SECRET

To remove fat from the liquid of cooked slow cooker dishes, first remove any solids from the liquid, let the liquid stand 5 minutes to allow the fat to surface, then skim off the fat with a large spoon.

Sauerbraten

1 boneless beef sirloin tip roast (1¼ pounds)
3 cups baby carrots
1½ cups fresh or frozen pearl onions
¼ cup raisins
½ cup water
½ cup red wine vinegar
1 tablespoon honey
½ teaspoon salt
½ teaspoon dry mustard
½ teaspoon garlic-pepper seasoning
¼ teaspoon ground cloves
¼ cup crushed crisp gingersnap cookies (5 cookies)

1. Heat large nonstick skillet over medium heat until hot. Brown roast on all sides; set aside.

2. Place roast, carrots, onions and raisins in slow cooker. Combine water, vinegar, honey, salt, mustard, garlic-pepper seasoning and cloves in large bowl; mix well. Pour mixture over meat and vegetables.

3. Cover; cook on LOW 4 to 6 hours or until internal temperature reaches 145°F when tested with meat thermometer inserted into thickest part of roast. Transfer roast to cutting board; cover with foil. Let stand 10 to 15 minutes before slicing. Internal temperature will continue to rise 5° to 10°F during stand time.

4. Remove vegetables with slotted spoon to bowl; cover to keep warm. Stir crushed cookies into sauce mixture in slow cooker. Cover; cook on HIGH 10 to 15 minutes or until sauce thickens. Serve meat and vegetables with sauce.   *Makes 5 servings*

Traci's 5-Layer Pot Roast

4 medium onions, cut into chunks, divided
1 package (16 ounces) frozen baby carrots, divided
6 celery stalks, cut into thirds, divided
  Garlic powder
  Salt
  Black pepper
  Water
1 large beef or pork roast, sliced in half horizontally
8 medium potatoes, peeled and cut into chunks
  All-purpose flour or cornstarch

1. Combine onions, carrots and celery in large bowl. Place ⅓ vegetable mixture in slow cooker. Season with garlic powder, salt and pepper to taste. Add water to cover.

2. Place bottom slice of roast on top of vegetables; season with garlic powder, salt and pepper. Top roast with ⅓ vegetables; season. Add top roast half; season. Top with remaining ⅓ vegetables; season well. Cover; cook on LOW 6 to 8 hours.

3. During last hour or two of cooking, add potatoes.

4. Serve with cooked juices from slow cooker. To make gravy, combine juices with flour in small saucepan. Cook and stir over medium heat until thickened. *Makes 8 to 10 servings*

Swiss Steak Stew

  ½ **cup all-purpose flour, divided**
  ½ **teaspoon salt**
1½ **pounds boneless beef round steak, cut into bite-size pieces**
    Nonstick cooking spray
  3 **cups peeled and quartered red potatoes**
  1 **medium onion, diced**
  1 **can (14½ ounces) Italian-style diced tomatoes, undrained**
  ¾ **cup water**
  1 **cup corn**

1. Combine ¼ cup flour and salt in large bowl. Add beef; stir to coat.

2. Coat nonstick skillet with cooking spray; heat over medium-low heat. Add beef; brown beef on all sides.

3. Layer potatoes, beef and onion in slow cooker. Combine tomatoes with juice, water and ¼ cup remaining flour in medium bowl. Pour over ingredients in slow cooker. Cover; cook on LOW 7 to 8 hours or until beef is tender.

4. Add corn. Cover; cook on LOW an additional 30 minutes. *Makes 6 servings*

SLOW COOKING SECRET
Browning meats and poultry before cooking in the slow cooker is not necessary but can enhance flavor and appearance of the finished dish.

Slow Cooker Pepper Steak

2 tablespoons vegetable oil
3 pounds sirloin steak, cut into strips
1 heaping tablespoon minced garlic (5 to 6 cloves)
1 medium onion, chopped
½ cup reduced-sodium soy sauce
2 teaspoons sugar
1 teaspoon salt
½ teaspoon ground ginger
½ teaspoon black pepper
3 green bell peppers, cut into strips
¼ cup cold water
1 tablespoon cornstarch
Hot cooked white rice

1. Heat oil in large skillet over medium-low heat. Brown steak strips; sprinkle with garlic.

2. Transfer meat and pan juices to slow cooker. Add onion, soy sauce, sugar, salt, ginger and black pepper; mix well. Cover; cook on LOW 6 to 8 hours or until meat is tender (up to 10 hours).

3. In final hour of cooking, add bell pepper strips. Before serving, mix together water and cornstarch; stir into slow cooker. Cook on HIGH 10 minutes or until thickened. Serve over hot rice.

Makes 6 to 8 servings

Slow Cooker Pepper Steak

Smothered Steak

1½ to 2 pounds beef cubed steaks
   All-purpose flour
1 can (10¾ ounces) condensed cream of mushroom soup
1 can (4 ounces) sliced mushrooms, drained
1 package (1 ounce) dry onion soup mix

Dust steak lightly with flour. Place in slow cooker. Combine mushroom soup, mushrooms and onion soup mix in medium bowl; pour over steak. Cover; cook on LOW 6 to 8 hours.

Makes 4 servings

Slow Cooker Hamburger Casserole

4 medium potatoes, thinly sliced
3 carrots, thinly sliced
1 can (15 ounces) green peas, drained
1 can (15 ounces) corn, drained
3 medium onions, chopped
1½ pounds extra-lean ground beef, browned and drained
   Salt
   Black pepper
1 can (10¾ ounces) condensed tomato soup
1 soup can water

Layer ingredients inside slow cooker in order listed, occasionally seasoning with salt and pepper. Cover with tomato soup and water. Cover; cook on LOW 6 to 8 hours or on HIGH 2 to 4 hours.

Makes 4 to 6 servings

Smothered Steak

Slow-Cooked Beef Brisket Dinner

1 beef brisket (4 pounds), cut in half
4 to 6 medium potatoes, cut into large chunks
6 carrots, cut into 1-inch pieces
8 ounces sliced mushrooms
½ large onion, sliced
1 rib celery, cut into 1-inch pieces
3 cubes beef bouillon
5 cloves garlic, crushed
1 teaspoon black peppercorns
2 bay leaves
   Water

1. Place all ingredients in slow cooker, adding enough water to cover ingredients. Cover; cook on LOW 6 to 8 hours. Remove and discard bay leaves

2. Remove brisket to cutting board. Slice across the grain and serve with vegetables.

Makes 8 to 10 servings

Four Layer Delight

    1½ teaspoons salt
    1½ teaspoons dried thyme leaves
     ¾ teaspoon black pepper
    ½ pound sliced bacon, cut into 1-inch pieces
     2 pounds beef round or chuck steak
     3 large russet potatoes, scrubbed and sliced
     2 large onions, thinly sliced

1. Combine salt, thyme and pepper in small bowl. set aside.

2. Sprinkle bacon pieces over bottom of slow cooker. Place steak on top of bacon; sprinkle with ½ seasoning mixture. Add potatoes and onions; sprinkle with remaining seasoning mixture. Cover, cook on LOW 8 hours.   *Makes 4 servings*

Note: There should be plenty of liquid in the cooker, but you may need to add some water after several hours of cooking.

Excellent Tailgating Beef & Noodles

    1 beef round steak (2 pounds), cubed
    2 jars (10 ounces each) beef gravy
    1 package (12 ounces) egg noodles, cooked according to package directions

1. Place steak cubes in slow cooker; cover with gravy. Cover; cook on LOW 8 to 10 hours.

2. To serve, spoon steak and gravy over noodles.   *Makes 4 to 6 servings*

Serving Suggestion: Serve with a tossed salad for a great, easy meal.

Swiss Steak

1 beef round steak (2 pounds), cut to fit into slow cooker
All-purpose flour
Salt
Black pepper
1 onion, sliced into thick rings
1 clove garlic, minced
1 can (28 ounces) whole tomatoes, undrained
1 can (10¾ ounces) condensed tomato soup
3 medium potatoes, unpeeled, diced
1 package (16 ounces) frozen peas and carrots
1 cup sliced celery
Additional vegetables

1. Dredge steak in flour seasoned with salt and pepper. Shake off excess flour.

2. Place onion and garlic in bottom of slow cooker. Add steak and tomatoes with juice. Cover with tomato soup. Add potatoes, peas and carrots, celery and any additional vegetables. Cover; cook on HIGH 4 to 6 hours or until meat and potatoes are tender.   *Makes 8 servings*

Variation: Substitute corn or green beans for peas and carrots.

Swiss Steak

Lemon-Thyme Beef with Beans

3 pounds beef chuck roast, trimmed and cut in 2-inch pieces
2 cans (15 ounces each) white or pinto beans, rinsed and drained
1 can (15 ounces) red kidney beans, rinsed and drained
1 cup beef broth
1 medium onion, chopped
2 cloves garlic, minced
1 teaspoon salt
1 teaspoon grated lemon peel
1 teaspoon dried thyme leaves
1 teaspoon black pepper
Chopped fresh parsley

1. Place beef, beans, broth, onion, garlic, salt, lemon peel, thyme and pepper into slow cooker. Cover; cook on LOW 8 to 9 hours.

2. Adjust seasonings before serving, if desired. Arrange beef on top of beans. Garnish with parsley.

Makes 6 to 8 servings

Slow Cooker Stew

1 pound beef for stew
1 package (1 ounce) au jus mix
2 cans (15 ounces each) beef broth
1 pound potatoes, peeled and diced
½ pound carrots, peeled and cut into 2-inch pieces *or* ½ pound baby carrots
2 medium onions, chopped
  Water
1 bag (16 ounces) frozen peas, thawed
1 tablespoon cornstarch

1. Place stew meat in slow cooker. Add au jus mix, broth, potatoes, carrots, onions and enough water to cover. Cover; cook on LOW 8 hours.

2. Add peas one hour before serving, .

3. Just before serving, sprinkle with cornstarch and stir. Cook 5 minutes to thicken sauce.

Makes 4 to 6 servings

Variation: Substitute a cut-up chicken for the stew meat and add chicken broth instead of beef broth. Omit the au jus mix for a delicious chicken stew.

Main-Dish Pork

Cajun-Style Country Ribs

2 cups baby carrots
1 large onion, coarsely chopped
1 large green bell pepper, cut into 1-inch pieces
1 large red bell pepper, cut into 1-inch pieces
2 teaspoons minced garlic
2 tablespoons Cajun or Creole seasoning mix, divided
3½ to 4 pounds country-style pork spareribs
1 can (14½ ounces) stewed tomatoes, undrained
2 tablespoons water
1 tablespoon cornstarch
Hot cooked rice

1. Place carrots, onion, bell peppers, garlic and 2 teaspoons seasoning mix in slow cooker; mix well. Trim excess fat from ribs. Cut into individual riblets. Sprinkle 1 tablespoon seasoning mix over ribs; place in slow cooker over vegetables. Pour tomatoes with juice over ribs (slow cooker will be full). Cover; cook on LOW 6 to 8 hours or until ribs are fork tender.

2. Remove ribs and vegetables from cooking liquid to serving platter. Let liquid stand 5 minutes to allow fat to rise. Skim off fat.

3. Blend water, cornstarch and remaining 1 teaspoon Cajun seasoning. Stir into liquid in slow cooker. Cook on HIGH until sauce is thickened. Return ribs and vegetables to sauce; carefully stirring to coat. Serve with rice. *Makes 6 servings*

Cajun-Style Country Ribs

Pork Meatballs & Sauerkraut

1¼ pounds lean ground pork
¾ cup dry bread crumbs
1 egg, slightly beaten
2 tablespoons milk
2 teaspoons caraway seeds, divided
1 teaspoon salt
½ teaspoon Worcestershire sauce
¼ teaspoon black pepper
1 bag (32 ounces) sauerkraut, drained, squeezed dry and snipped
½ cup chopped onion
6 slices bacon, crisp-cooked and crumbled
Chopped parsley

1. Combine ground pork, bread crumbs, egg, milk, 1 teaspoon caraway seeds, salt, Worcestershire and pepper in large bowl. Shape mixture into 2-inch balls. Brown meatballs in large nonstick skillet over medium-high heat.

2. Combine sauerkraut, onion, bacon and remaining 1 teaspoon caraway seeds in slow cooker. Place meatballs on top of sauerkraut mixture. Cover; cook on LOW 6 to 8 hours. Garnish with chopped parsley.   *Makes 4 to 6 servings*

Pork Meatballs & Sauerkraut

Sweet & Saucy Ribs

2 pounds pork baby back ribs
1 teaspoon black pepper
2½ cups barbecue sauce (not mesquite flavored)
1 jar (8 ounces) cherry jam or preserves
1 tablespoon Dijon mustard
¼ teaspoon salt
Additional salt and black pepper (optional)

1. Trim excess fat from ribs. Rub 1 teaspoon black pepper over ribs. Cut ribs into 2-rib portions; place into slow cooker.

2. Combine barbecue sauce, jam, mustard and salt in small bowl; pour over ribs. Cover; cook on LOW 6 to 8 hours or until ribs are tender. Season with additional salt and pepper, if desired. Serve ribs with sauce. *Makes 4 servings*

Peking Pork Chops

6 pork chops, about 1 inch thick
½ cup soy or teriyaki sauce
¼ cup brown sugar
¼ cup Chinese ketchup or ketchup
1 teaspoon ground ginger
1 to 2 cloves garlic, crushed
Salt
Black pepper

1. Trim excess fat from pork chops. Place chops into slow cooker.

2. Combine soy sauce, brown sugar, ketchup, ginger and garlic in small bowl; pour over meat. Cover; cook on LOW 4 to 6 hours or until pork is tender. Season with salt and pepper, if desired. *Makes 6 servings*

Sweet & Saucy Ribs

Ham Meat Loaf with Horseradish Sauce

1½ pounds meat loaf mix* or ground beef
½ pound cooked ham, finely chopped
1 cup plain dry bread crumbs
1 cup finely chopped onion
2 large eggs, slightly beaten
½ cup chili sauce or ketchup
1 teaspoon plus ⅛ teaspoon salt, divided
½ teaspoon caraway seeds
¼ teaspoon black pepper
½ cup sour cream
3 tablespoons thinly sliced green onions
1 tablespoon prepared horseradish
1 tablespoon spicy brown or coarse-grained mustard

*Meat loaf mix is a combination of ground beef, pork and veal; see your meat retailer or make your own with 1 pound lean ground beef, ¼ pound ground pork and ¼ pound ground veal.

1. Combine meat loaf mix, ham, bread crumbs, onion, eggs, chili sauce, 1 teaspoon salt, caraway seeds and pepper in large bowl; mix well. Shape meat mixture into 7-inch round loaf.

2. Make foil handles using technique described below. Place meat loaf on top of foil strips. Using strips, place meat loaf into slow cooker. Cover; cook on LOW 4 to 4½ hours or until meat thermometer inserted into center of meat loaf reads 165°F. Use foil strips to remove meat loaf from slow cooker. Let stand 5 minutes.

3. Meanwhile, combine sour cream, green onions, horseradish, mustard and remaining ⅛ teaspoon salt in small bowl; mix well. Cut meat loaf into wedges; serve with horseradish sauce.   *Makes 8 servings*

Foil Handles: Tear off three 18 x 2-inch strips of heavy foil or use regular foil folded to double thickness. Crisscross foil strips in spoke design as shown on page 7.

Autumn Harvest Sausage and Cabbage

1 package (12 ounces) reduced-fat pork sausage
8 cups chopped red cabbage (1 small head)
3 potatoes, diced
3 apples, diced
1 onion, sliced
½ cup sugar
½ cup white vinegar
1 teaspoon salt
½ teaspoon black pepper
½ teaspoon ground allspice
¼ teaspoon ground cloves

1. Cook sausage in large nonstick skillet over medium-high heat until no longer pink, stirring to separate; drain fat.

2. Combine sausage and remaining ingredients in large bowl; mix well. Spoon mixture into slow cooker. Cover; cook on LOW 8 to 10 hours or until potatoes are tender.

Makes 6 to 8 servings

Note: It is easier to mix all the ingredients in a large bowl instead of the slow cooker because the slow cooker will be filled to the top until the cabbage cooks down.

Shredded Pork Wraps

1 cup salsa, divided
2 tablespoons cornstarch
1 bone-in pork sirloin roast (2 pounds)
6 (8-inch) flour tortillas
3 cups broccoli slaw mix
⅓ cup shredded reduced-fat Cheddar cheese

1. Combine ¼ cup salsa and cornstarch in small bowl; stir until smooth. Pour mixture into slow cooker. Top with pork roast. Pour remaining ¾ cup salsa over roast.

2. Cover; cook on LOW 6 to 8 hours or until internal temperature reaches 165°F when tested with meat thermometer inserted in thickest part of roast, not touching bone. Transfer roast to cutting board; cover with foil and let stand 10 to 15 minutes or until cool enough to handle. (Internal temperature will rise 5° to 10°F during stand time.) Trim and discard outer fat from pork. Using 2 forks, pull pork into coarse shreds.

3. Divide shredded meat evenly among tortillas. Spoon about 2 tablespoons salsa mixture on top of meat in each tortilla. Top evenly with broccoli slaw and cheese. Fold bottom edge of tortilla over filling; fold in sides. Roll up completely to enclose filling. Serve remaining salsa mixture as dipping sauce.

Makes 6 servings

Shredded Pork Wrap

Cantonese Pork

    1 tablespoon vegetable oil
    2 pounds pork tenderloin, cut into strips
    1 can (8 ounces) pineapple tidbits
    1 can (8 ounces) tomato sauce
    2 cans (4 ounces each) sliced mushrooms, drained
    1 medium onion, thinly sliced
    3 tablespoons brown sugar
    2 tablespoons Worcestershire sauce
  1½ teaspoons salt
  1½ teaspoons white vinegar
    Hot cooked rice

1. Heat oil in large nonstick skillet over medium-low heat. Brown pork on all sides. Drain excess fat.

2. Place all ingredients into slow cooker. Cover; cook on HIGH 4 hours or on LOW 6 to 8 hours.

3. Serve over rice.

Makes 8 servings

SLOW COOKING SECRET

Most manufacturers recommend that slow cookers be one-half to three-quarters full for the best results.

Cantonese Pork

Cajun Sausage and Rice

8 ounces kielbasa sausage, cut in ¼-inch slices
1 can (14½ ounces) diced tomatoes, undrained
1 medium onion, diced
1 medium green bell pepper, diced
2 ribs celery, thinly sliced
1 tablespoon chicken bouillon granules
1 tablespoon steak sauce
3 bay leaves *or* 1 teaspoon dried thyme leaves
1 teaspoon sugar
¼ to ½ teaspoon hot pepper sauce
1 cup uncooked instant rice
½ cup water
½ cup chopped parsley (optional)

1. Combine sausage, tomatoes with juice, onion, bell pepper, celery, bouillon, steak sauce, bay leaves, sugar and hot pepper sauce in slow cooker. Cover; cook on LOW 8 hours or on HIGH 4 hours.

2. Remove bay leaves; stir in rice and water. Cook on HIGH 25 minutes or until rice is done. Stir in parsley, if desired. *Makes 5 servings*

Hearty White Beans and Ham

1 package (16 ounces) dried navy beans or mixed dried beans
  Water
1 meaty ham bone
1 can (14½ ounces) tomatoes with green chilies, undrained
1 medium potato, diced
1 stalk celery, diced
½ small onion, diced
½ envelope dried onion soup mix
1 tablespoon Worcestershire sauce
1 teaspoon salt
½ teaspoon black pepper

1. Sort, rinse and drain beans. Place in Dutch oven; cover with water. Bring to a boil; reduce heat and simmer 1 hour. Drain water from beans; return to soup pot. Add ham bone and enough water to cover generously. Cook 1 to 2 hours over low heat. Remove ham bone; pull meat from bone.

2. Transfer beans, liquid, ham bone and meat to slow cooker. Add remaining ingredients; mix well. Cover; cook on LOW 6 to 8 hours or until beans are done. Remove and discard ham bone.   *Makes 10 servings*

Barbecued Pulled Pork

3 to 4 pound boneless pork shoulder or butt roast
1 teaspoon salt
1 teaspoon ground cumin
1 teaspoon paprika
1 teaspoon black pepper
½ teaspoon ground red pepper
1 medium onion, thinly sliced
1 medium green bell pepper, cut into strips
1 bottle (18 ounces) barbecue sauce
½ cup packed light brown sugar
Hot cooked rice
Flour tortillas

1. Trim excess fat from pork. Combine salt, cumin, paprika, black pepper and red pepper in small bowl; rub over roast.

2. Place onion and bell pepper in slow cooker; add pork. Combine barbecue sauce and brown sugar; pour over meat. Cover; cook on LOW 8 to 10 hours.

3. Transfer roast to cutting board. Trim and discard fat from roast. Using 2 forks, pull pork into coarse shreds.

4. Serve pork and sauce over rice with tortillas.

Makes 4 to 6 servings

Barbecued Pulled Pork

Panama Pork Stew

2 small sweet potatoes, peeled and cut into 2-inch pieces
(about 12 ounces total)
1 package (10 ounces) frozen corn
1 package (9 ounces) frozen cut green beans
1 cup chopped onion
1¼ pounds lean pork stew meat, cut into 1-inch cubes
1 can (14½ ounces) diced tomatoes, undrained
¼ cup water
1 to 2 tablespoons chili powder
½ teaspoon salt
½ teaspoon ground coriander

1. Place potatoes, corn, green beans and onion in slow cooker. Top with pork.

2. Combine tomatoes with juice, water, chili powder, salt and coriander in large bowl. Pour over pork in slow cooker. Cover; cook on LOW 7 to 9 hours.   *Makes 6 servings*

SLOW COOKING SECRET

To remove a small amount of fat from dishes cooked in the slow cooker, lightly pull a sheet of clean paper towel over the surface, letting the grease be absorbed by the paper towel. Repeat this process if necessary.

Panama Pork Stew

Ham and Potato Casserole

1½ pounds red potatoes, peeled and sliced
8 ounces thinly sliced ham
2 poblano chili peppers, cut into thin strips
2 tablespoons olive oil
1 tablespoon dried oregano leaves
¼ teaspoon salt
1 cup (4 ounces) shredded Monterey Jack cheese with or without hot peppers
2 tablespoons finely chopped fresh cilantro

1. Combine all ingredients except cheese and cilantro in slow cooker; mix well. Cover; cook on LOW 7 hours or on HIGH 4 hours.

2. Transfer potato mixture to serving dish; sprinkle with cheese and cilantro. Let stand 3 minutes or until cheese melts.

Makes 6 to 7 servings

Lemon Pork Chops

1 tablespoon vegetable oil
4 boneless pork chops
3 cans (8 ounces each) tomato sauce
1 large onion, quartered and sliced
1 large green bell pepper, cut into strips
1 tablespoon lemon-pepper seasoning
1 tablespoon Worcestershire sauce
1 large lemon, quartered

1. Heat oil in large skillet over medium-low heat. Brown pork chops on both sides. Drain excess fat. Place pork in slow cooker.

2. Combine tomato sauce, onion, bell pepper, lemon-pepper seasoning and Worcestershire sauce in slow cooker. Squeeze juice from lemon quarters over mixture; drop squeezed peels into slow cooker. Cover; cook on LOW 6 to 8 hours or until pork is tender. Remove and discard lemon peels.

Makes 4 servings

Peachy Pork

2 cans (about 15 ounces each) sliced peaches in heavy syrup, undrained
6 to 8 boneless pork blade or top loin chops (about 2 pounds)
1 small onion, thinly sliced
½ cup golden raisins
¼ cup packed light brown sugar
3 tablespoons cider vinegar
2 tablespoons tapioca
1 teaspoon salt
¾ teaspoon cinnamon
¼ teaspoon red pepper flakes
2 tablespoons cornstarch
2 tablespoons water

1. Cut peach slices in half with spoon. Place peaches with juice, pork chops, onion, raisins, sugar, vinegar, tapioca, salt, cinnamon and pepper flakes into slow cooker. Cover; cook on LOW 7 to 8 hours.

2. Remove pork to warm platter. Skim off fat from peach mixture. Combine cornstarch and water to make smooth paste. Stir into peach mixture. Cook on HIGH 15 minutes or until sauce is thickened. Adjust seasonings, if desired.   *Makes 7 to 8 hours*

Red Beans and Rice with Ham

1 package (1 pound) dried red beans
1 pound beef smoked sausage, sliced
1 ham slice, cubed (about 8 ounces)
1 small onion, diced
2½ to 3 cups water
1 teaspoon adobo seasoning with pepper
⅛ teaspoon ground red pepper
Hot cooked rice

1. Soak beans overnight; rinse and drain.

2. Place beans in slow cooker. Add sausage, ham, onion and water (3 cups for HIGH; 2½ cups for LOW). Season with adobo seasoning and pepper.

3. Cover; cook on HIGH 3 to 4 hours or on LOW 7 to 8 hours or until beans are done, stirring every 2 hours, if necessary.

4. Serve over rice.   *Makes 6 servings*

SLOW COOKING SECRET

Recipes often provide a range of cooking times in order to account for variables such as the temperature of the ingredients before cooking, the quantity of food in the slow cooker and the altitude.

Red Beans and Rice with Ham

Italian-Style Sausage with Rice

1 pound mild Italian sausage, cut in 1-inch pieces
1 can (29 ounces) pinto beans, rinsed and drained
1 cup spaghetti sauce
1 green bell pepper, cut into strips
1 small onion, halved and sliced
½ teaspoon salt
¼ teaspoon black pepper
   Hot cooked rice
   Chopped fresh basil

1. Brown sausage in large nonstick skillet over medium heat. Pour off drippings. Place sausage, beans, spaghetti sauce, bell pepper, onion, salt and pepper into slow cooker. Cover; cook on LOW 4 to 6 hours.

2. Serve with rice. Garnish with basil, if desired.   *Makes 4 to 5 servings*

Ham & Potato Scallop

8 slices ham
4 medium potatoes, thinly sliced
1 large onion, sliced
   Salt
   Black pepper
1 cup corn
1 can (10¾ ounces) condensed cream of mushroom soup
1 cup (4 ounces) shredded Cheddar cheese
1 tablespoon Worcestershire sauce

1. Layer ham, potatoes and onion in slow cooker; season with salt and pepper. Add corn.

2. Combine soup, cheese and Worcestershire sauce in medium bowl. Pour over ham mixture. Cover; cook on LOW 8 hours or until potatoes are done.   *Makes 8 servings*

Italian-Style Sausage with Rice

Two White Meats Together
(Marinated Pork and Chicken)

6 pounds boneless chicken pieces
2 pounds lean boneless pork, cubed
6 cups beef broth
2 cups sherry or apple juice
6 Roma tomatoes, chopped
2 teaspoons salt
4 cloves garlic, crushed
1 teaspoon dried rosemary leaves
1 teaspoon black pepper

1. Place chicken and pork in large bowl. To make marinade, combine remaining ingredients in large bowl. Pour half of marinade mixture over chicken and pork. Cover bowl; marinate meat in refrigerator 4 hours or overnight. Cover remaining marinade; refrigerate.

2. Drain and discard marinade from meats. Place meats into slow cooker. Add remaining marinade. Cover; cook on LOW 6 to 8 hours or until meat is tender. Adjust seasonings, if desired.

Makes 12 servings

Golden Harvest Pork Stew

1 pound boneless pork cutlets, cut into 1-inch pieces
2 tablespoons all-purpose flour, divided
1 tablespoon vegetable oil
2 medium Yukon gold potatoes, unpeeled and cut into 1-inch cubes
1 large sweet potato, peeled and cut into 1-inch cubes
1 cup chopped carrots
1 ear corn, broken into 4 pieces *or* ½ cup corn
½ cup chicken broth
1 jalapeño pepper, seeded and finely chopped
1 clove garlic, minced
1 teaspoon salt
¼ teaspoon black pepper
¼ teaspoon dried thyme leaves

1. Toss pork pieces with 1 tablespoon flour; set aside. Heat oil in large nonstick skillet over medium-high heat until hot. Brown pork 2 to 3 minutes per side; transfer to 5-quart slow cooker.

2. Add remaining ingredients to slow cooker. Cover; cook on LOW 5 to 6 hours.

3. Combine remaining 1 tablespoon flour and ¼ cup broth from stew in small bowl; stir until smooth. Stir flour mixture into stew. Cook on HIGH 10 minutes or until thickened. Adjust seasonings, if desired.

Makes 4 to 5 servings

SLOW COOKING SECRET

Trim excess fat from meat before putting in the slow cooker to help reduce the fat.

Honey Ribs

1 can (10¾ ounces) condensed beef consommé
½ cup water
3 tablespoons soy sauce
2 tablespoons honey
2 tablespoons maple syrup
2 tablespoons barbecue sauce
½ teaspoon dry mustard
2 pounds extra-lean baby back ribs

1. Combine all ingredients except ribs in slow cooker; mix well.

2. Add ribs to slow cooker. (If ribs are especially fatty, broil 10 minutes before adding to slow cooker.) Cover; cook on LOW 6 to 8 hours or on HIGH to 4 hours or until ribs are tender.

Makes 4 servings

Simple Slow Cooker Pork Roast

4 to 5 red potatoes, cut into bite-size pieces
4 carrots, cut into bite-size pieces
1 marinated pork roast (any size)
½ cup water
1 package (10 ounces) frozen baby peas, thawed

1. Place potatoes, carrots and pork roast into slow cooker. Add water. Cover; cook on LOW 6 to 8 hours or until vegetables are done.

2. Add peas during last hour of cooking. Adjust seasonings, if desired. *Makes 6 servings*

Honey Ribs

Pork and Mushroom Ragout

> 1 boneless pork loin roast (1¼ pounds)
> 1¼ cups canned crushed tomatoes, divided
> 2 tablespoons cornstarch
> 2 teaspoons dried savory leaves
> 3 sun-dried tomatoes, chopped
> 1 package (8 ounces) sliced mushrooms
> 1 large onion, sliced
> 1 teaspoon black pepper
> 3 cups hot cooked noodles

1. Spray large nonstick skillet with nonstick cooking spray; heat skillet over medium heat until hot. Brown roast on all sides; set aside.

2. Place ½ cup crushed tomatoes, cornstarch, savory and sun-dried tomatoes into slow cooker; mix well. Layer mushrooms, onion and roast over tomato mixture.

3. Pour remaining tomatoes over roast; sprinkle with pepper. Cover; cook on LOW 4 to 6 hours or until internal temperature reaches 165°F when tested with meat thermometer inserted into the thickest part of roast.

4. Transfer roast to cutting board; cover with foil. Let stand 10 to 15 minutes. Internal temperature will continue to rise 5° to 10°F during stand time.

5. Slice roast. Serve with sauce over hot cooked noodles.   *Makes 6 servings*

Pork and Mushroom Ragout

Orange Teriyaki Pork

   1 pound lean pork stew meat, cut into 1-inch cubes
   1 package (16 ounces) frozen pepper blend for stir-fry
   4 ounces sliced water chestnuts
   ½ cup orange juice
   2 tablespoons quick-cooking tapioca
   2 tablespoons packed light brown sugar
   2 tablespoons teriyaki sauce
   ½ teaspoon ground ginger
   ½ teaspoon dry mustard
1⅓ cups hot cooked rice

1. Spray large nonstick skillet with nonstick cooking spray; heat skillet over medium heat until hot. Add pork; brown on all sides. Remove from heat; set aside.

2. Place peppers and water chestnuts in slow cooker. Top with browned pork. Mix orange juice, tapioca, brown sugar, teriyaki sauce, ginger and mustard in large bowl. Pour over pork mixture in slow cooker. Cover; cook on LOW 3 to 4 hours.

3. Serve with rice. *Makes 4 servings*

SLOW COOKING SECRET

Slow cooking may take longer in high altitudes. Allow an additional 30 minutes for each hour of cooking time specified in the recipe.

Sauerkraut Pork Ribs

  1 tablespoon vegetable oil
  3 to 4 pounds country-style pork ribs
  1 large onion, thinly sliced
  1 teaspoon caraway seeds
  ½ teaspoon garlic powder
  ¼ to ½ teaspoon black pepper
  ¾ cup water
  1 jar (about 28 ounces) sauerkraut
  6 medium potatoes, quartered

1. Heat oil in large skillet over medium-low heat. Brown ribs on all sides; transfer ribs to slow cooker. Drain excess fat.

2. Add onion to skillet; cook until tender. Add caraway seeds, garlic powder and pepper; cook 15 minutes. Transfer onion mixture to slow cooker. Add water to skillet and scrape bottom of pan. Pour pan juices into slow cooker.

3. Partially drain sauerkraut, leaving some liquid; pour over meat in slow cooker. Top with potatoes. Cover; cook on LOW 6 to 8 hours or until potatoes are tender, mixing once during cooking.   *Makes 12 servings*

Pork & Tomato Ragout

2 pounds pork stew meat, cut into 1-inch pieces
¼ cup all-purpose flour
3 tablespoons oil
1¼ cups white wine
2 pounds red potatoes, cut into ½-inch pieces
1 can (14½ ounces) diced tomatoes, undrained
1 cup finely chopped onion
1 cup water
½ cup finely chopped celery
2 cloves garlic, minced
½ teaspoon black pepper
1 cinnamon stick
3 tablespoons chopped fresh parsley

1. Toss pork with flour. Heat oil in large skillet over medium-high heat. Add pork to skillet and brown on all sides. Place pork into slow cooker.

2. Add wine to skillet; bring to a boil, scraping up browned bits from bottom of skillet. Pour into slow cooker.

3. Add all remaining ingredients except parsley. Cover; cook on LOW 6 to 8 hours or until pork and potatoes are tender. Remove and discard cinnamon stick. Adjust seasonings, if desired. Sprinkle with parsley just before serving. *Makes 6 servings*

Pork & Tomato Ragout

Mediterranean Meatball Ratatouille

2 tablespoons olive oil, divided
1 pound bulk mild Italian sausage
1 package (8 ounces) sliced mushrooms
1 small eggplant, diced
1 zucchini, diced
½ cup chopped onion
1 clove garlic, minced
1 teaspoon dried oregano leaves, divided
1 teaspoon salt, divided
½ teaspoon black pepper, divided
2 tomatoes, diced
1 tablespoon tomato paste
2 tablespoons chopped fresh basil
1 teaspoon fresh lemon juice

1. Pour 1 tablespoon olive oil into 5-quart slow cooker. Shape sausage into 1-inch meatballs. Place half the meatballs in slow cooker. Add half the mushrooms, eggplant, zucchini. Top with onion, garlic, ½ teaspoon oregano, ½ teaspoon salt and ¼ teaspoon pepper.

2. Add remaining meatballs, mushrooms, eggplant and zucchini, ½ teaspoon oregano, ½ teaspoon salt and ¼ teaspoon pepper. Top with remaining 1 tablespoon olive oil. Cover; cook on LOW 6 to 7 hours.

3. Stir in diced tomatoes and tomato paste. Cover; cook on LOW 15 minutes. Stir in basil and lemon; serve.

Makes 6 (1⅖ cups) servings

Curried Pork Pot

   1 can (10¾ ounces) condensed cream of chicken soup
   1 cup evaporated skimmed milk or water
   1 medium onion, chopped
  ½ cup raisins
   1 tablespoon mild curry powder
   1 tablespoon dried parsley
   1 teaspoon minced garlic
   1 pound boneless country-style pork ribs
     Salt
     Black pepper
     Hot cooked rice, pasta or egg noodles

1. Combine soup, milk, onion, raisins, curry, parsley and garlic in large bowl; mix well. Add pork, stirring to coat.

2. Pour mixture into slow cooker. Cover; cook on LOW 6 to 8 hours or on HIGH 4 to 6 hours. Stir in salt and pepper to taste.

3. Serve over rice, pasta or noodles.

Makes 6 servings

SLOW COOKING SECRET

Always taste the finished dish before serving. Adjust the seasoning to your preference by adding a small amount of salt, pepper, herbs and spices from the original recipe.

Easy Pork Chop Dinner

1 large onion, thinly sliced
3 to 4 medium baking potatoes, sliced
6 pork chops
1 can (10¾ ounces) reduced-fat condensed cream of celery soup
½ cup water or milk

1. Place onion then potatoes into slow cooker. Top with pork.

2. Combine soup and water in small bowl; pour over chops. Cover; cook on LOW 6 to 8 hours.   *Makes 6 servings*

Chili Verde

1 tablespoon vegetable oil
1 to 2 pounds boneless pork chops
   Sliced carrots (enough to cover bottom of slow cooker)
1 jar (24 ounces) mild green chili salsa
   Chopped onion (optional)

1. Heat oil in large skillet over medium-low heat. Brown pork on all sides. Drain excess fat.

2. Place carrot slices in bottom of slow cooker. Place pork on top of carrots. Pour salsa over chops. Add onion to taste, if desired. Cover; cook on HIGH 6 to 8 hours. Shred the pork and serve with tortillas, if desired.   *Makes 4 to 8 servings*

Simply Delicious Pork

1½ pounds boneless pork loin, sliced
4 medium Yellow Delicious apples, sliced
3 tablespoons brown sugar
1 teaspoon cinnamon
½ teaspoon salt

Place pork slices in bottom of slow cooker. Cover with apples. Combine brown sugar, cinnamon and salt in small bowl; sprinkle over apples. Cover; cook on LOW 6 to 8 hours.

Makes 6 servings

Slow-Cooked Pork Chops

1 teaspoon vegetable oil
6 pork chops
1 can (10¾ ounces) condensed cream of mushroom soup
1 can (10¾ ounces) condensed cream of celery soup
1 tablespoon beef bouillon granules
Salt
Black pepper

1. Heat oil in large skillet over medium-low heat. Brown pork on both sides. Drain excess fat. Place pork into slow cooker.

2. Combine all ingredients in medium bowl; pour over pork. Cover; cook on LOW 6 hours or until pork is tender. Adjust seasonings, if desired. Serve over rice or mashed potatoes.

Makes 6 servings

Simply Delicious Pork

Sweet and Sour Spare Ribs

    4 pounds pork spare ribs
    2 cups dry sherry or chicken broth
    ½ cup pineapple, mango or guava juice
    ⅓ cup chicken broth
    2 tablespoons packed light brown sugar
    2 tablespoons cider vinegar
    2 tablespoons soy sauce
    1 clove garlic, minced
    ½ teaspoon salt
    ¼ teaspoon black pepper
    ⅛ teaspoon red pepper flakes
    2 tablespoons cornstarch

1. Preheat oven to 400°F. Place ribs in foil-lined shallow roasting pan. Bake 30 minutes, turning over after 15 minutes. Remove from oven. Slice meat into 2-rib portions. Place ribs in 5-quart slow cooker. Add remaining ingredients except cornstarch to slow cooker.

2. Cover; cook on LOW 6 hours. Transfer ribs to platter; keep warm. Let liquid in slow cooker stand 5 minutes to allow fat to rise. Skim off fat.

3. Combine cornstarch and ¼ cup liquid from slow cooker; stir until smooth. Stir mixture into liquid in slow cooker; mix well. Cook on HIGH 10 minutes or until slightly thickened.

Makes 4 servings

Sweet and Sour Spare Ribs

Succulent Pork Chops

2 teaspoons olive oil
6 boneless pork chops, ½ inch thick
1 can (10¾ ounces) condensed cream of chicken soup
1 can (10¾ ounces) condensed cream of mushroom soup
1 can (8 ounces) sliced mushrooms, drained
1 cup milk
2 teaspoons minced garlic
   Salt
   Black pepper

1. Heat oil in large skillet over medium-low heat. Brown pork chops on both sides. Drain excess fat.

2. Place pork chops in slow cooker. Add remaining ingredients over top. Cover; cook on LOW 8 to 10 hours or on HIGH 5 to 7 hours. Adjust seasonings, if desired.

Makes 6 servings

SLOW COOKING SECRET

Do not use the slow cooker to reheat left-over foods. Transfer any cooled leftover food to a resealable plastic food-storage bag or plastic storage container with a tight-fitting lid and refrigerate. Use a microwave oven, the range top or oven for reheating.

Buck County Ribs

    4 boneless country-style pork ribs
    1 teaspoon salt
    1 jar (about 28 ounces) sauerkraut, drained
    1 medium apple, diced
    1 tablespoon sugar
    1 teaspoon chicken bouillon granules *or* 1 cup chicken broth
    Mashed potatoes (optional)

1. Place ribs into slow cooker. Sprinkle with salt. Spoon sauerkraut over ribs. Top with apple; sprinkle sugar over apple. Add bouillon granules. Cover; cook on LOW 8 to 9 hours.

2. Serve with mashed potatoes, if desired.   *Makes 4 servings*

Fall Apart Pork Chops

    2 teaspoons vegetable oil
    4 center cut bone-in pork chops
    1 can (10¾ ounces) condensed cream of mushroom soup
    ¼ cup water
    ¼ cup cooking wine (such as sherry or marsala) or apple juice

1. Heat oil in large skillet over medium-low heat. Brown pork chops on both sides; season as desired. Drain excess fat. Transfer pork chops to slow cooker.

2. Whisk together soup, water and wine in large bowl. Pour mixture over top or pork. Cover; cook on HIGH 3 hours or until meat is tender. (Cook longer for very thick chops.)

    Makes 4 servings

MAKE-AHEAD POULTRY

Mexicali Chicken

2 medium green bell peppers, cut into thin strips
1 large onion, quartered and thinly sliced
4 chicken thighs
4 chicken drumsticks
1 tablespoon chili powder
2 teaspoons dried oregano leaves
1 jar (16 ounces) chipotle salsa
½ cup ketchup
2 teaspoons ground cumin
½ teaspoon salt
Hot cooked noodles

1. Place bell peppers and onion in slow cooker; top with chicken. Sprinkle chili powder and oregano evenly over chicken. Add salsa. Cover; cook on LOW 7 to 8 hours or until chicken is tender.

2. Remove chicken pieces to serving bowl; keep warm. Stir ketchup, cumin and salt into liquid in slow cooker. Cook, uncovered, on HIGH 15 minutes or until hot.

3. Pour mixture over chicken. Serve with noodles.   *Makes 4 servings*

Helpful Hint: For thicker sauce, blend 1 tablespoon cornstarch and 2 tablespoons water. Stir into cooking liquid with ketchup, cumin and salt.

Mexicali Chicken

Turkey with Pecan-Cherry Stuffing

1 fresh or frozen boneless turkey breast (about 3- to 4-pounds)
2 cups cooked rice
⅓ cup chopped pecans
⅓ cup dried cherries or cranberries
1 teaspoon poultry seasoning
¼ cup peach, apricot or plum preserves
1 teaspoon Worcestershire sauce

1. Thaw turkey breast, if frozen. Remove and discard skin. Cut slices three fourths of the way through turkey at 1-inch intervals.

2. Stir together rice, pecans, cherries and poultry seasoning in large bowl. Stuff rice between slices. If needed, skewer turkey lengthwise to hold together.

3. Place turkey in slow cooker. Cover; cook on LOW 5 to 6 hours or until turkey registers 170°F on meat thermometer inserted into thickest part of breast, not touching stuffing.

4. Stir together preserves and Worcestershire sauce. Spoon over turkey. Cover; let stand for 5 minutes. Remove and discard skewer, if used. *Makes 8 servings*

Turkey with Pecan-Cherry Stuffing

Chicken with Italian Sausage

10 ounces bulk mild or hot Italian sausage
6 boneless skinless chicken thighs
1 can (about 15 ounces) white beans, rinsed and drained
1 can (about 15 ounces) red beans, rinsed and drained
1 cup chicken broth
1 medium onion, chopped
1 teaspoon black pepper
½ teaspoon salt
Chopped fresh parsley

1. Brown sausage in large skillet over medium-high heat, stirring to separate; drain fat. Spoon into slow cooker.

2. Trim fat from chicken. Place chicken, beans, broth, onion, pepper and salt in slow cooker. Cover; cook on LOW 5 to 6 hours.

3. Adjust seasonings, if desired. Slice each chicken thigh on the diagonal. Serve with sausage and beans. Garnish with parsley, if desired. *Makes 6 servings*

SLOW COOKING SECRET
To reduce the amount of fat in slow cooker meals, degrease canned broths.

Turkey with Chunky Cherry Relish

1 bag (16 ounces) frozen dark cherries, coarsely chopped
1 can (14 ounces) diced tomatoes with jalapeños, undrained
1 package (6 ounces) dried cherry-flavored cranberries or dried cherries, coarsely chopped
2 small onions, thinly sliced
1 small green bell pepper, chopped
½ cup packed brown sugar
2 tablespoons tapioca
1½ tablespoons salt
½ teaspoon ground cinnamon
½ teaspoon black pepper
½ bone-in turkey breast (about 2½ to 3 pounds)
2 tablespoons water
1 tablespoon cornstarch

1. Place cherries, tomatoes with juice, cranberries, onions, bell pepper, brown sugar, tapioca, salt, cinnamon and black pepper in slow cooker; mix well.

2. Place turkey on top of mixture. Cover; cook on LOW 7 to 8 hours or until turkey registers 170°F on meat thermometer inserted into thickest part of breast, not touching bone.

3. Remove turkey from slow cooker; keep warm. Combine water and cornstarch to form smooth paste. Stir into cherry mixture. Cook, uncovered on HIGH 15 minutes or until thickened. Adjust seasoning, if desired. Slice turkey and top with relish.

Makes 4 to 6 servings

Slow-Simmered Curried Chicken

1½ cups chopped onions
1 medium green bell pepper, chopped
1 pound boneless skinless chicken breast or thighs, cut into bite-size pieces
1 cup medium salsa
2 teaspoons grated fresh ginger
½ teaspoon garlic powder
½ teaspoon red pepper flakes
¼ cup chopped fresh cilantro
1 teaspoon sugar
1 teaspoon curry powder
¾ teaspoon salt
Hot cooked rice

1. Place onions and bell pepper in bottom of slow cooker. Top with chicken. Combine salsa, ginger, garlic powder and pepper flakes in small bowl; spoon over chicken. Cover; cook on LOW 5 to 6 hours or until chicken is tender.

2. Combine cilantro, sugar, curry powder and salt in small bowl. Stir mixture into slow cooker. Cover; cook on HIGH 15 minutes or until hot.

3. Serve with rice.

Makes 4 servings

Slow-Simmered Curried Chicken

Cheesy Slow Cooker Chicken

6 boneless skinless chicken breasts
Salt
Black pepper
Garlic powder
2 cans (10¾ ounces each) condensed cream of chicken soup
1 can (10¾ ounces) condensed Cheddar cheese soup
Chopped fresh parsley (optional)

1. Place 3 chicken breasts in slow cooker. Sprinkle with salt, pepper and garlic powder. Repeat with remaining three breasts.

2. Mix soups together in medium bowl; pour over chicken. Cover; cook on LOW 6 to 8 hours. Garnish with parsley before serving, if desired. *Makes 6 servings*

Orange Chicken

1 pound boneless skinless chicken breasts
1 can (12 ounces) orange soda
½ cup soy sauce
Hot cooked rice

1. Place all ingredients except rice in slow cooker. Cover; cook on LOW 5 to 6 hours.

2. Serve over rice. *Makes 4 servings*

Cheesy Slow Cooker Chicken

Tender Asian-Style Chicken

6 to 8 boneless skinless chicken thighs
¼ cup flour
½ teaspoon black pepper
1 tablespoon vegetable oil
¼ cup soy sauce
2 tablespoons rice wine vinegar
2 tablespoons ketchup
1 tablespoon brown sugar
1 clove garlic, minced
½ teaspoon grated fresh ginger or ¼ teaspoon ground ginger
¼ teaspoon red pepper flakes
Hot cooked rice
Chopped fresh cilantro (optional)

1. Trim visible fat from chicken. Combine flour and pepper in resealable plastic food storage bag. Add chicken; shake to coat with flour mixture.

2. Heat oil in large skillet over medium-high heat. Add chicken and brown about 2 minutes on each side. Place chicken in slow cooker.

3. Combine soy sauce, vinegar, ketchup, sugar, garlic, ginger and red pepper flakes in small bowl; pour over chicken. Cook on LOW 5 to 6 hours.

4. Serve with rice and garnish with cilantro, if desired.   *Makes 4 to 6 servings*

Sweet Jalapeño Mustard Turkey Thighs

    3 turkey thighs, skin removed
    ¾ cup honey mustard
    ½ cup orange juice
    1 tablespoon cider vinegar
    1 teaspoon Worcestershire sauce
    1 to 2 fresh jalapeño peppers,* finely chopped
    1 clove garlic, minced
    ½ teaspoon grated orange peel

*Jalapeño peppers can sting and irritate the skin; wear rubber gloves when handling peppers and do not touch eyes. Wash hands after handling.

Place turkey thighs in single layer in slow cooker. Combine remaining ingredients in large bowl. Pour mixture over turkey thighs. Cover; cook on LOW 5 to 6 hours.

Makes 6 servings

SLOW COOKING SECRET

Skinless turkey is best for the slow cooker because the skin tends to shrivel and curl during cooking.

Greek-Style Chicken

6 boneless skinless chicken thighs
½ teaspoon salt
½ teaspoon black pepper
1 tablespoon olive oil
½ cup chicken broth
1 lemon, thinly sliced
¼ cup pitted kalamata olives
½ teaspoon dried oregano leaves
1 clove garlic, minced
Hot cooked orzo or rice

1. Remove visible fat from chicken; sprinkle chicken with salt and pepper. Heat oil in large skillet over medium-high heat. Brown chicken on all sides. Place chicken in slow cooker.

2. Add broth, lemon, olives, oregano and garlic to slow cooker. Cover; cook on LOW 5 to 6 hours or until chicken is tender.

3. Serve with orzo.   *Makes 4 to 6 servings*

Greek-Style Chicken

Continental Chicken

1 package (2¼ ounces) dried beef, cut up
4 boneless skinless chicken breasts
4 slices lean bacon
1 can (10¾ ounces) condensed cream of mushroom soup
¼ cup all-purpose flour
¼ cup low-fat sour cream
Hot cooked noodles

1. Spray slow cooker cooking surface with nonstick cooking spray. Place dried beef in bottom of slow cooker. Wrap each piece of chicken with one bacon strip. Place wrapped chicken on top of dried beef.

2. Combine soup, flour and sour cream in medium bowl until smooth. Pour over chicken. Cover; cook on LOW 7 to 9 hours or on HIGH 3 to 4 hours.

3. Serve over noodles. *Makes 4 servings*

SLOW COOKING SECRET

One hour on HIGH equals 2 to 2½ hours on LOW for slow cookers that have the heat coils circling the crockery insert.

Continental Chicken

Southwestern-Style Chicken

6 to 8 boneless skinless chicken thighs or breasts
1 package (about 1¼ ounces) taco seasoning mix
¼ cup flour
2 tablespoons vegetable oil
1 large onion, cut into 1-inch pieces
2 green peppers, cut into 1-inch pieces
1 can (14½ ounces) diced tomatoes with jalapeños, undrained
   Salt and pepper

1. Trim visible fat from chicken.

2. Reserve one teaspoon taco seasoning. Combine flour and remaining seasoning in plastic food storage bag. Add chicken, 1 to 2 pieces at a time; shake to coat.

3. Heat oil in large skillet over medium-high heat; brown chicken. Transfer chicken to slow cooker; sprinkle with reserved seasoning.

4. Add onion to skillet; cook and stir until translucent. Transfer onion to slow cooker. Top with green peppers and tomatoes with juice. Cover; cook on LOW 6 to 7 hours or until chicken is tender. Season with salt and pepper to taste. *Makes 4 to 6 servings*

Black Bean and Turkey Stew

    3 cans (15 ounces each) black beans, drained and rinsed
1½ cups chopped onions
1½ cups fat-free reduced-sodium chicken broth
    1 cup sliced celery
    1 cup chopped red bell pepper
    4 cloves garlic, minced
1½ teaspoons dried oregano leaves
    ¾ teaspoon ground coriander
    ½ teaspoon ground cumin
    ¼ teaspoon ground red pepper
    6 ounces cooked turkey sausage, thinly sliced

1. Combine all ingredients in slow cooker, except sausage. Cover; cook on LOW 6 to 8 hours.

2. Transfer about 1½ cups bean mixture from slow cooker to blender or food processor; purée bean mixture. Return to slow cooker. Stir in sausage. Cover; cook on LOW an additional 10 to 15 minutes.   *Makes 6 servings*

SLOW COOKING SECRET

Sprinkle diced fresh tomatoes or snipped fresh herbs over slow cooker soups and stews to enhance color and flavor.

French Country Slow Cooker Chicken

1 medium onion, chopped
4 carrots, sliced
4 celery stalks, sliced
6 to 8 boneless skinless chicken breasts
1 teaspoon dried tarragon leaves
1 teaspoon dried thyme leaves
   Salt and black pepper, to taste
1 can (10¾ ounces) condensed cream of chicken soup
1 envelope (1 ounce) dried onion soup mix
⅓ cup white wine or apple juice
2 tablespoons cornstarch
   Hot cooked rice

1. Place onion, carrots and celery in bottom of slow cooker. Arrange chicken over vegetables. Sprinkle chicken with tarragon, thyme, salt and pepper. Pour soup over chicken. Sprinkle with onion soup mix. Cover; cook on HIGH 3 to 4 hours, stirring once.

2. Twenty minutes before serving, whisk together wine and cornstarch in small bowl. Stir until smooth. Pour mixture over chicken; stir well. Cook, uncovered, on HIGH 15 minutes or until sauce thickens.

3. Serve over rice.

Makes 6 servings

French Country Slow Cooker Chicken

Saucy Tropical Turkey

1 small onion, halved and sliced
3 to 4 turkey thighs, skin removed (about 2½ pounds)
2 tablespoons cooking oil
1 can (20 ounces) pineapple chunks, drained
1 red bell pepper, cubed
⅔ cup apricot preserves
3 tablespoons soy sauce
1 teaspoon grated lemon peel
1 teaspoon ground ginger
¼ cup cold water
2 tablespoons cornstarch
Hot cooked rice or noodles

1. Place onion in slow cooker.

2. Rinse turkey and pat dry. Heat oil in large skillet; brown turkey on all sides. Transfer to slow cooker and top with pineapple and bell pepper.

3. Combine preserves, soy sauce, lemon peel and ginger in small bowl; mix well. Spoon over turkey. Cover; cook on LOW 6 to 7 hours.

4. Remove turkey from slow cooker; keep warm. Blend water and cornstarch until smooth; stir into slow cooker. Cook on HIGH 15 minutes or until sauce is slightly thickened. Adjust seasonings, if desired. Return turkey to slow cooker; cook until hot.

5. Serve with rice.

Makes 6 servings

Country Captain Chicken

4 boneless skinless chicken thighs
2 tablespoons all-purpose flour
2 tablespoons vegetable oil, divided
1 cup chopped green bell pepper
1 large onion, chopped
1 rib celery, chopped
1 clove garlic, minced
¼ cup chicken broth
2 cups canned or fresh crushed tomatoes
½ cup golden raisins
1½ teaspoons curry powder
1 teaspoon salt
¼ teaspoon paprika
¼ teaspoon black pepper
2 cups hot cooked rice

1. Coat chicken with flour; set aside. Heat 1 tablespoon oil in large skillet over medium-high heat until hot. Add bell pepper, onion, celery and garlic. Cook and stir 5 minutes or until vegetables are tender. Place vegetables in slow cooker.

2. Heat remaining 1 tablespoon oil in same skillet over medium-high heat. Add chicken; cook 5 minutes per side. Place chicken in slow cooker.

3. Pour broth into skillet. Heat over medium-high heat, stirring frequently and scraping up any browned bits from bottom of skillet. Pour liquid into slow cooker. Add tomatoes, raisins, curry powder, salt, paprika and black pepper. Cover; cook on LOW 3 hours.

4. Serve chicken with sauce over rice. *Makes 4 servings*

Gypsy's BBQ Chicken

6 boneless skinless chicken breasts
1 bottle (26 ounces) barbecue sauce
6 slices bacon
6 slices Swiss cheese

1. Place chicken in slow cooker. Cover with barbecue sauce. Cover; cook on LOW 8 to 9 hours.

2. Before serving, cut bacon strips in half. Cook bacon in microwave or on stovetop, keeping bacon flat.

3. Place 2 strips cooked bacon over each piece of chicken in slow cooker. Top with cheese slices. Cover; cook on HIGH until cheese melts.   *Makes 6 servings*

Note: If juices become too thick during cooking, add a little water.

SLOW COOKING SECRET

Do not cook whole chickens in the slow cooker because the temperature of the chicken cannot reach the desired level quickly enough for food safety.

Slow Cooker Chicken & Rice

3 cans (10¾ ounces each) condensed cream of chicken soup
2 cups quick-cooking rice
1 cup water
1 pound boneless skinless chicken breasts or breast tenders
½ teaspoon salt
¼ teaspoon black pepper
¼ teaspoon paprika
½ cup diced celery

Combine soup, rice and water in slow cooker. Add chicken; sprinkle with salt, pepper and paprika. Sprinkle celery over top of chicken. Cover; cook on HIGH 3 to 4 hours or on LOW 6 to 8 hours.

Makes 4 servings

SLOW COOKING SECRET

When adapting your own recipes for the slow cooker, use canned evaporated milk, nonfat dry milk or condensed soups instead of milk to make smooth sauces.

Slow Cooker Chicken & Rice

Chicken Parisienne

6 boneless skinless chicken breasts, cubed
½ teaspoon salt
½ teaspoon black pepper
½ teaspoon paprika
1 can (10¾ ounces) condensed cream of mushroom or cream of chicken soup
2 cans (4 ounces each) sliced mushrooms, drained
½ cup dry white wine
1 cup sour cream
6 cups hot cooked egg noodles

1. Place chicken in slow cooker. Sprinkle with salt, pepper and paprika.

2. Add soup, mushrooms and wine to slow cooker; mix well. Cover; cook on HIGH 2 to 3 hours. In last 30 minutes of cooking, add sour cream.

3. Serve over noodles. Garnish as desired.

Makes 6 servings

SLOW COOKING SECRET

Dairy products should be added at the end of the cooking time, because they will curdle if cooked in the slow cooker for a long time.

Chicken Parisienne

Bonnie's Slow-Cooked Turkey Thighs with Potatoes

1 large onion, sliced
2 turkey thighs, skin removed
2 cloves garlic, minced
½ teaspoon black pepper
8 to 10 small red potatoes
1 can (12 ounces) beer *or* 1½ cups chicken broth
1 can (8 ounces) tomato sauce
1 bay leaf

Place onion slices on bottom of slow cooker. Place turkey thighs over onions; sprinkle with garlic and pepper. Place potatoes around turkey thighs. Add beer, tomato sauce and bay leaf. Cover; cook on LOW 8 to 10 hours. Remove and discard bay leaf. *Makes 2 to 4 servings*

Kat's Slow Chicken

1 cut-up whole chicken (3 pounds)
1 jar (26 ounces) spaghetti sauce
1 medium onion, sliced
1 medium green bell pepper, cut into strips
2 medium potatoes, cubed
1 carrot, sliced
1 rib celery, sliced
4 cloves garlic, minced
½ cup water

Combine all ingredients in slow cooker. Cover; cook on LOW 6 to 8 hours.

Makes 4 servings

Southwestern Turkey in Chilies and Cream

1 can (15 ounces) corn, drained
1 can (4 ounces) diced green chilies, drained
1 boneless skinless turkey breast, cut into 1-inch pieces
2 tablespoons plus 2 teaspoons flour, divided
1 tablespoon butter
½ cup chicken broth
1 clove garlic, minced
1 teaspoon salt
½ teaspoon paprika
¼ teaspoon dried oregano leaves
¼ teaspoon black pepper
½ cup heavy cream
2 tablespoons chopped fresh cilantro
3 cups hot cooked rice or pasta

1. Place corn and green chilies in slow cooker.

2. Coat turkey pieces with 2 tablespoons flour. Melt butter in large nonstick skillet over medium heat. Add turkey pieces; brown on all sides. Place turkey in slow cooker. Add broth, garlic, salt, paprika, oregano and pepper. Cover; cook on LOW 2 hours or until turkey is tender and no longer pink in center.

3. Combine cream and remaining 2 teaspoons flour in small bowl, stirring until smooth. Pour mixture into slow cooker. Cover; cook on HIGH 10 minutes or until slightly thickened. Stir in cilantro.

4. Serve over rice.

Makes 6 (1½-cup) servings

Mu Shu Turkey

1 can (16 ounces) plums, drained, rinsed and pitted
½ cup orange juice
¼ cup finely chopped onion
1 tablespoon minced fresh ginger
¼ teaspoon ground cinnamon
1 pound boneless turkey breast, cut into thin strips
6 (7-inch) flour tortillas
3 cups coleslaw mix

1. Place plums in blender or food processor. Cover and blend until almost smooth. Combine plums, orange juice, onion, ginger and cinnamon in slow cooker; mix well. Place turkey over plum mixture. Cover; cook on LOW 3 to 4 hours.

2. Remove turkey from slow cooker and divide evenly among tortillas. Spoon about 2 tablespoons plum sauce over turkey in each tortilla; top with about ½ cup coleslaw mix. Fold bottom edge of tortilla over filling; fold in sides. Roll up to completely enclose filling. Repeat with remaining tortillas. Use remaining plum sauce for dipping. *Makes 6 servings*

Mu Shu Turkey

Moroccan Chicken Tagine

3 pounds chicken, cut into serving pieces and skin removed
2 cups chicken broth
1 can (14½ ounces) diced tomatoes, undrained
2 onions, chopped
1 cup dried apricots, chopped
4 cloves garlic, minced
2 teaspoons ground cumin
1 teaspoon ground cinnamon
1 teaspoon ground ginger
½ teaspoon ground coriander
½ teaspoon ground red pepper
6 sprigs fresh cilantro
1 tablespoon cornstarch
1 tablespoon water
1 can (15 ounces) chick-peas, drained and rinsed
2 tablespoons chopped fresh cilantro
¼ cup slivered almonds, toasted
   Hot cooked couscous or rice

1. Place chicken in slow cooker. Combine broth, tomatoes with juice, onions, apricots, garlic, cumin, cinnamon, ginger, coriander, red pepper and cilantro sprigs in medium bowl; pour over chicken. Cover; cook on LOW 4 to 5 hours or until chicken is no longer pink in center. Transfer chicken to serving platter; cover to keep warm.

2. Combine cornstarch and water in small bowl; mix until smooth. Stir cornstarch mixture and chick-peas into slow cooker. Cover; cook on HIGH 15 minutes or until sauce is thickened. Pour sauce over chicken. Sprinkle with almonds and cilantro. Serve with couscous.

Makes 4 to 6 servings

Helpful Hint: To toast almonds, heat small nonstick skillet over medium-high heat. Add almonds; cook and stir about 3 minutes or until golden brown. Remove from pan at once. Let cool before adding to other ingredients.

Moroccan Chicken Tagine

Chicken and Chile Pepper Stew

1 pound boneless skinless chicken thighs, cut into ½-inch pieces
1 pound small potatoes, cut lengthwise in halves and then cut crosswise
    into slices
1 cup chopped onion
2 poblano chile peppers, seeded and cut into ½-inch pieces
1 jalapeño pepper,* seeded and finely chopped
3 cloves garlic, minced
3 cups fat-free reduced-sodium chicken broth
1 can (14½ ounces) no-salt-added diced tomatoes, undrained
2 tablespoons chili powder
1 teaspoon dried oregano leaves

*Jalapeño peppers can sting and irritate the skin; wear rubber gloves when handling peppers and do not touch eyes. Wash hands after handling.

1. Place chicken, potatoes, onion, poblano peppers, jalapeño pepper and garlic into slow cooker.

2. Stir together broth, tomatoes with juice, chili powder and oregano in large bowl. Pour broth mixture over chicken mixture in slow cooker; mix well. Cover; cook on LOW 8 to 9 hours.

Makes 6 servings

SLOW COOKING SECRET

Use freshly ground pepper for a quick simple flavor enhancer for slow cooker dishes.

My Favorite Chicken

   1 cut-up whole chicken (about 3 pounds)
   1 cup chopped onion
   1 cup sliced celery
   1 cup sliced carrots
   ½ teaspoon seasoning salt
   ½ teaspoon black pepper
   ¼ teaspoon garlic powder
   ¼ teaspoon poultry seasoning
   3 to 4 medium potatoes, sliced
   1 can (14 ounces) chicken broth

Place chicken pieces, onion, celery, carrots, seasoning salt, garlic powder, poultry seasoning and pepper into slow cooker. Top with potatoes. Pour broth over top. Cover; cook on HIGH 30 minutes. Turn to LOW; cook 6 to 8 hours.   *Makes 4 servings*

Note: Use a slotted spoon and transfer solids to a bowl. Thicken the juice left in the slow cooker with a mixture of cornstarch and water.

Hot & Sour Chicken

4 to 6 boneless skinless chicken breasts
1 envelope (1 ounce) dried hot-and-sour soup mix
1 cup chicken or vegetable broth

Place chicken in slow cooker. Add soup mix and broth. Cover; cook on LOW 5 to 6 hours. Garnish as desired. *Makes 4 to 6 servings*

Serving Suggestions: Serve over steamed white rice and topped with crispy Chinese noodles. Or, for a colorful variation, serve it over a bed of snow peas and sugar snap peas tossed with diced red bell pepper.

Nice 'n' Easy Italian Chicken

1 pound boneless skinless chicken breasts
1 medium onion, chopped
8 ounces mushrooms, sliced
1 medium green bell pepper, chopped (optional)
1 medium zucchini, diced
1 jar (26 ounces) favorite spaghetti sauce

Combine all ingredients in slow cooker. Cover; cook on LOW 6 to 8 hours.

Makes 4 servings

Hot & Sour Chicken

Creamy Chicken and Mushrooms

       1 teaspoon salt
     ½ teaspoon black pepper
     ¼ teaspoon paprika
       3 boneless skinless chicken breasts, cut up
    1½ cups sliced fresh mushrooms
     ½ cup sliced green onions
    1¾ teaspoons chicken bouillon granules
       1 cup white wine
     ½ cup water
       1 can (5 ounces) evaporated milk
       5 teaspoons cornstarch
         Hot cooked rice

1. Combine salt, pepper and paprika in small bowl; sprinkle over chicken.

2. Layer chicken, mushrooms, green onions and bouillon in slow cooker. Pour wine and water over top. Cover; cook on HIGH 3 hours or on LOW 5 to 6 hours. Remove chicken and vegetables to platter; cover to keep warm.

3. Combine evaporated milk and cornstarch in small saucepan, stirring until smooth. Add 2 cups liquid from slow cooker; bring to a boil. Boil 1 minute or until thickened, stirring constantly.

4. Serve chicken over rice and top with sauce.   *Makes 3 to 4 servings*

Creamy Chicken and Mushrooms

Old World Chicken and Vegetables

1 tablespoon dried oregano leaves
1 teaspoon salt, divided
1 teaspoon paprika
½ teaspoon garlic powder
¼ teaspoon black pepper
2 medium green bell peppers, cut into thin strips
1 small yellow onion, thinly sliced
1 cut-up whole chicken (3 pounds)
⅓ cup ketchup
6 ounces uncooked egg noodles

1. Combine oregano, ½ teaspoon salt, paprika, garlic powder and black pepper in small bowl; mix well.

2. Place bell peppers and onion in slow cooker. Top with chicken thighs and legs, sprinkle with half the oregano mixture, top with chicken breasts. Sprinkle chicken with remaining oregano mixture. Cover; cook on LOW 8 hours or on HIGH 4 hours. Stir in ketchup and remaining ½ teaspoon salt.

3. Just before serving, cook noodles following package directions; drain. Serve chicken and vegetables over noodles.   *Makes 4 servings*

Chicken Azteca

 2 cups frozen corn
 1 can (15 ounces) black beans, rinsed and drained
 1 cup chunky salsa, divided
 1 clove garlic, minced
 ½ teaspoon ground cumin
 4 boneless skinless chicken breasts
 1 package (8 ounces) cream cheese, cubed
   Hot cooked rice
   Shredded Cheddar cheese

1. Combine corn, beans, ½ cup salsa, garlic and cumin in slow cooker. Arrange chicken breasts over top; pour remaining ½ cup salsa over chicken. Cover; cook on HIGH 2 to 3 hours or on LOW 4 to 6 hours or until chicken is tender.

2. Remove chicken; cut into bite-size pieces. Return chicken to slow cooker; add cream cheese. Cook on HIGH until cream cheese melts and blends into sauce.

3. Spoon chicken and sauce over rice. Top with Cheddar cheese. *Makes 4 servings*

SLOW COOKING SECRET
Skinless chicken is best for the slow cooker because the skin tends to shrivel and curl during cooking.

Heidi's Chicken Supreme

1 can (10¾ ounces) condensed cream of chicken soup
1 envelope (1 ounce) dried onion soup mix
6 boneless skinless chicken breasts
½ cup canned bacon crumbles *or* **½ pound bacon, crisp-cooked and crumbled**
1 carton (16 ounces) reduced-fat sour cream

1. Spray slow cooker cooking surface with nonstick cooking spray. Combine soup with dried soup mix in medium bowl; mix well. Layer chicken breasts and soup mixture in slow cooker. Sprinkle with bacon crumbles.

2. Cover; cook on HIGH 4 hours or on LOW 8 hours. During last hour of cooking, stir in sour cream. *Makes 6 servings*

Heather's Chicken Tetrazzini

4 to 6 boneless skinless chicken breasts
Garlic salt
Lemon-pepper seasoning
1 can (10¾ ounces) condensed cream of chicken soup
1 can (10¾ ounces) condensed cream of broccoli soup
1 package (16 ounces) spaghetti
Grated Parmesan cheese (optional)

1. Place chicken in slow cooker; sprinkle with garlic salt and lemon-pepper seasoning to taste. Pour soups over top. Cover; cook on LOW 6 to 8 hours.

2. Before serving, cook spaghetti according to package directions; drain. Serve chicken over spaghetti. Sprinkle with grated Parmesan cheese, if desired. *Makes 4 to 6 servings*

Heidi's Chicken Supreme

Spicy Shredded Chicken

6 boneless skinless chicken breasts
1 jar of your favorite prepared salsa

Place chicken in slow cooker. Cover with salsa. Cover; cook on LOW 6 to 8 hours. Shred chicken with two forks before serving. *Makes 6 servings*

Serving Suggestion: Serve on warm flour tortillas with taco toppings

Creamy Chicken

3 boneless skinless chicken breasts *or* 6 boneless skinless thighs
2 cans (10¾ ounces each) condensed cream of chicken soup
1 can (14½ ounces) chicken broth
1 can (4 ounces) mushrooms, drained
½ medium onion, diced
   Salt to taste
   Black pepper to taste

Place all ingredients in slow cooker. Cover; cook on LOW 6 to 8 hours. *Makes 3 servings*

Variation: Add cubed American processed cheese food before serving.

Spicy Shredded Chicken

Chicken Cacciatore

¼ **cup vegetable oil**
2½ **to 3 pounds chicken pieces**
1 **can (28 ounces) crushed Italian-style tomatoes**
2 **cans (8 ounces each) Italian-style tomato sauce**
1 **medium onion, chopped**
1 **can (4 ounces) sliced mushrooms, drained**
2 **cloves garlic, minced**
1 **teaspoon salt**
1 **teaspoon dried oregano leaves**
½ **teaspoon dried thyme leaves**
½ **teaspoon black pepper**
 Hot cooked spaghetti or rice

1. Heat oil in large skillet over medium-low heat. Brown chicken on all sides. Drain excess fat.

2. Transfer chicken to slow cooker. Add remaining ingredients except spaghetti. Cover; cook on LOW 6 to 8 hours.

3. Serve over spaghetti.   *Makes 6 to 8 servings*

Turkey Breast with Barley-Cranberry Stuffing

2 cups fat-free reduced-sodium chicken broth
1 cup quick-cooking barley
½ cup chopped onion
½ cup dried cranberries
2 tablespoons slivered almonds, toasted
½ teaspoon rubbed sage
½ teaspoon garlic-pepper seasoning
1 fresh or frozen bone-in turkey breast half (about 2 pounds), thawed and skinned
⅓ cup finely chopped fresh parsley

1. Combine broth, barley, onion, cranberries, almonds, sage and garlic-pepper seasoning in slow cooker.

2. Spray large nonstick skillet with nonstick cooking spray. Heat over medium heat until hot. Brown turkey breast on all sides; add to slow cooker. Cover; cook on LOW 3 to 4 hours or until internal temperature reaches 170°F when tested with meat thermometer inserted into the thickest part of breast, not touching bone.

3. Transfer turkey to cutting board; cover with foil and let stand 10 to 15 minutes before carving. Internal temperature will rise 5° to 10°F during stand time.

4. Stir parsley into sauce mixture in slow cooker. Serve sauce with sliced turkey.

Makes 6 servings

Herbed Turkey Breast with Orange Sauce

1 large onion, chopped
3 cloves garlic, minced
1 teaspoon dried rosemary
½ teaspoon black pepper
2 to 3 pounds boneless skinless turkey breast
1½ cups orange juice
2 tablespoons water
1 tablespoon cornstarch

1. Place onion in slow cooker. Combine garlic, rosemary and pepper in small bowl; set aside. Cut slices about three fourths of the way through turkey at 2-inch intervals. Rub garlic mixture between slices.

2. Place turkey, cut side up, in slow cooker. Pour orange juice over turkey. Cover; cook on LOW 7 to 8 hours or until internal temperature reaches 170°F when tested with meat thermometer inserted into the thickest part of breast, not touching bone.

3. Transfer turkey to cutting board; cover with foil and let stand 10 to 15 minutes before carving. Internal temperature will rise 5° to 10°F during stand time.

4. Combine water and cornstarch, stirring until smooth. Stir into slow cooker juices. Cook on HIGH 15 minutes or until thickened. Serve sauce with sliced turkey.   *Makes 4 to 6 servings*

SLOW COOKING SECRET
Defrost meats and vegetables before cooking them in the slow cooker.

Herbed Turkey Breast with Orange Sauce

Sweet Chicken Curry

1 pound boneless skinless chicken breasts, cut into 1-inch pieces
1 large green or red bell pepper, cut into 1-inch pieces
1 large onion, sliced
1 large tomato, seeded and chopped
½ cup prepared mango chutney
¼ cup water
2 tablespoons cornstarch
1½ teaspoons curry powder
1⅓ cups hot cooked rice

1. Place chicken, bell pepper and onion in slow cooker. Top with tomato.

2. Mix chutney, water, cornstarch and curry powder in small bowl. Pour chutney mixture over chicken mixture into slow cooker. Cover; cook on LOW 3½ to 4½ hours.

3. Serve over rice.   *Makes 4 servings*

SLOW COOKING SECRET

Slow cooker recipes with raw meats should cook a minimum of 3 hours on LOW and reach an internal temperature of 165°F or above.

Sweet Chicken Curry

Nicole's Favorite Slow Cooker Chicken Cacciatore

  6 boneless skinless chicken breasts
    Garlic powder
    Onion powder
    Seasoned salt
    Italian seasoning
    Black pepper
 10 ounces mushrooms, sliced
  1 can (15 ounces) Italian-style tomato sauce
 ¼ cup red wine or chicken broth
  8 ounces bow-tie pasta, cooked

1. Spray slow cooker with cooking spray for easy cleanup. Place chicken in slow cooker. Sprinkle generously with seasonings to taste.

2. Add mushrooms. Pour tomato sauce and wine over top. Cover; cook on LOW 6 hours.

3. Serve with cooked pasta.

Makes 6 servings

Slow Cooker Chicken and Dressing

4 boneless skinless chicken breasts
Salt
Black pepper
4 slices Swiss cheese
1 can (14½ ounces) chicken broth
2 cans (10¾ ounces each) condensed cream of chicken or celery or
    mushroom soup
3 cups packaged stuffing mix
½ cup butter, melted

1. Place chicken in bottom of slow cooker. Season with salt and pepper to taste.

2. Top each breast with cheese slice. Add broth and soups. Sprinkle stuffing mix over top; pour melted butter over all. Cover; cook on LOW 6 to 8 hours or on HIGH 3 to 4 hours.

Makes 4 servings

SLOW COOKING SECRET

When cooking in the slow cooker, the lower temperatures lessen the chance of scorching and burning foods.

Chicken and Stuffing

½ **cup flour**
¾ **teaspoon seasoned salt**
¾ **teaspoon black pepper**
 4 to 6 boneless skinless chicken breasts
¼ **cup butter**
 2 cans (10¾ ounces each) condensed cream of mushroom soup
½ **cup water**
 1 package (12 ounces) seasoned stuffing mix

1. Combine flour, seasoned salt and pepper in large resealable food storage bag. Dredge chicken in flour mixture. Melt butter in large skillet over medium heat. Brown both sides of chicken. Transfer chicken to slow cooker.

2. Mix together soup and water in medium bowl; pour soup mixture over top of chicken.

3. Follow package directions for stuffing, decreasing liquid by half. Add to slow cooker over chicken. Cover; cook on HIGH 3 to 4 hours.   *Makes 4 to 6 servings*

Chicken Teriyaki

  1 pound boneless skinless chicken tenders
  1 can (6 ounces) pineapple juice
  ¼ cup soy sauce
  1 tablespoon sugar
  1 tablespoon minced fresh ginger
  1 tablespoon minced garlic
  1 tablespoon vegetable oil
  1 tablespoon molasses
 24 cherry tomatoes (optional)
  2 cups hot cooked rice

1. Combine all ingredients except rice in slow cooker. Cover; cook on LOW 2 hours or until chicken is tender.

2. Serve chicken and sauce over rice.

Makes 4 servings

SLOW COOKING SECRET

When adapting your favorite recipe to a slow cooker, you will want to reduce the liquid by as much as half, because slow-cooker cooking doesn't lose as much moisture as conventional cooking.

Turkey Spaghetti Sauce

    1 tablespoon vegetable oil
    2 pounds ground turkey
    1 can (12 ounces) beer
    1 jar (26 ounces) spaghetti sauce
    1 can (6 ounces) tomato paste
    1 envelope (1½ ounces) dried spaghetti sauce seasoning mix
      Water

1. Heat oil in large skillet over medium-low heat. Brown turkey, stirring to separate. Add beer; continue cooking until turkey is no longer pink.

2. Place turkey mixture in slow cooker. Add spaghetti sauce. Fill emptied sauce jar with water to rinse out remaining sauce. Pour jar full of water into slow cooker. Add tomato paste and dried spaghetti sauce seasoning mix. Cover; cook on LOW 6 to 8 hours.   *Makes 8 servings*

SLOW COOKING SECRET

Avoid putting a hot slow cooker insert directly on a very cold surface. The insert could crack from the shock of the two extreme temperatures.

Coconut Chicken Curry

- **1 tablespoon vegetable oil**
- **4 boneless skinless chicken breasts**
- **3 medium potatoes, peeled and chopped**
- **1 medium onion, sliced**
- **1 can (14 ounces) coconut milk**
- **1 cup chicken broth**
- **1½ teaspoons curry powder**
- **1 teaspoon hot pepper sauce (optional)**
- **½ teaspoon salt**
- **½ teaspoon black pepper**
- **1 package (10 ounces) frozen peas**
- **Hot cooked rice (optional)**

1. Heat oil in medium skillet over medium-high heat. Brown chicken breasts on both sides. Place potatoes and onion in slow cooker. Top with chicken breasts.

2. Combine coconut milk, broth, curry powder, pepper sauce, if desired, salt and pepper in medium bowl. Pour over chicken. Cover; cook on LOW 6 to 8 hours.

3. About 30 minutes before serving, add peas to slow cooker.

4. Serve over hot cooked rice, if desired.   *Makes 4 servings*

Coconut Chicken Curry

MEATLESS MEALS

Mushroom Barley Stew

  1 tablespoon olive oil
  1 medium onion, finely chopped
  1 cup chopped carrots (about 2 carrots)
  1 clove garlic, minced
  1 cup pearled barley
  1 cup dried wild mushrooms, broken into pieces
  1 teaspoon salt
  ½ teaspoon black pepper
  ½ teaspoon dried thyme leaves
  5 cups vegetable broth

1. Heat oil in medium skillet over medium-high heat. Add onion, carrots and garlic; cook and stir 5 minutes or until tender. Place into slow cooker.

2. Add barley, mushrooms, salt, pepper and thyme. Sir in broth. Cover; cook on LOW 6 to 7 hours. Adjust seasonings, if desired. *Makes 4 to 6 servings*

Variation: To turn this thick robust stew into a soup, add 2 to 3 additional cups of broth. Cook the same length of time.

Mushroom Barley Stew

Layered Mexican-Style Casserole

2 cans (15½ ounces each) hominy, drained
1 can (15 ounces) black beans, rinsed and drained
1 can (14½ ounces) diced tomatoes with garlic, basil and oregano, undrained
1 cup thick and chunky salsa
1 can (6 ounces) tomato paste
½ teaspoon ground cumin
3 large (about 9-inch diameter) flour tortillas
2 cups (8 ounces) shredded Monterey Jack cheese
¼ cup sliced black olives

1. Prepare foil handles (see below.) Place into slow cooke to make lifting of tortilla stack easier. Spray slow cooker with nonstick cooking spray.

2. Combine hominy, beans, tomatoes with juice, salsa, tomato paste and cumin in large bowl.

3. Press one tortilla in the bottom of slow cooker. (Edges of tortilla may turn up slightly.) Top with one third of the hominy mixture and one third of cheese. Repeat layers. Press remaining tortilla on top. Top with remaining hominy mixture. Set aside remaining cheese.

4. Cover; cook on LOW 6 to 8 hours. Sprinkle with remaining cheese and olives. Cover, let stand 5 minutes. Pull out with foil handles. *Makes 6 servings*

Note: Hominy is corn that has been treated with slaked lime to remove the germ and hull. It can be found with the canned vegetables in most supermarkets.

Foil Handles: Tear off three 18×2-inch strips of heavy foil or use regular foil folded to double thickness. Crisscross foil strips in spoke design as shown on page 7.

Caribbean Sweet Potato & Bean Stew

2 medium sweet potatoes (about 1 pound), peeled and cut into 1-inch cubes
2 cups frozen cut green beans
1 can (15 ounces) black beans, rinsed and drained
1 can (14½ ounces) vegetable broth
1 small onion, sliced
2 teaspoons Caribbean or Jamaican jerk seasoning
½ teaspoon dried thyme leaves
¼ teaspoon ground cinnamon
¼ teaspoon salt
⅓ cup slivered almonds, toasted*
    Hot pepper sauce (optional)

To toast almonds, spread in single layer on baking sheet. Bake in preheated 350°F oven 8 to 10 minutes or until golden brown, stirring frequently.

1. Combine all ingredients except almonds and hot pepper sauce in slow cooker. Cover; cook on LOW 5 to 6 hours or until vegetables are tender.

2. Adjust seasonings. Serve with almonds and hot pepper sauce, if desired.

Makes 4 servings

SLOW COOKING SECRET

Leave the peel on slow-cooked vegetables to keep the shape and nutrients. Scrub the skins of potatoes and carrots, then chop and add to the slow cooker.

Caribbean Sweet Potato & Bean Stew

Three Pepper Pasta Sauce

1 *each* red, yellow and green bell pepper, cut into 1-inch pieces
2 cans (14½ ounces each) diced tomatoes, undrained
1 cup chopped onion
1 can (6 ounces) tomato paste
4 cloves garlic, minced
2 tablespoons olive oil
1 teaspoon dried basil leaves
1 teaspoon dried oregano leaves
½ teaspoon salt
¼ teaspoon red pepper flakes or ground black pepper
Hot cooked pasta
Shredded Parmesan or Romano cheese

1. Combine all ingredients except pasta and cheese in slow cooker. Cover; cook on LOW 7 to 8 hours or until vegetables are tender.

2. Adjust seasonings, if desired. Serve with pasta and cheese.   *Makes 4 to 6 servings*

Helpful Hint: 3 cups mixed bell pepper chunks from a salad bar may be substituted for peppers.

Three Pepper Pasta Sauce

Southwestern Corn and Beans

1 tablespoon olive oil
1 large onion, diced
1 or 2 jalapeño peppers,* diced
1 clove garlic, minced
2 cans (16 ounces) light red kidney beans, rinsed and drained
1 bag (16 ounces) frozen corn
1 can (14½ ounces) diced tomatoes, undrained
1 green bell pepper, cut into 1-inch pieces
2 teaspoons medium-hot chili powder
¾ teaspoon salt
½ teaspoon ground cumin
½ teaspoon black pepper
1 carton (8 ounces) plain yogurt (optional)
Sliced black olives (optional)

*Jalapeño peppers can sting and irritate the skin; wear rubber gloves when handling peppers and do not touch eyes. Wash hands after handling.

1. Heat oil in medium skillet over medium heat. Add onion, jalapeño pepper and garlic; cook 5 minutes. Add onion mixture, kidney beans, corn, tomatoes with juice, bell pepper, chili powder, salt, cumin and black pepper to slow cooker. Cover; cook on LOW 7 to 8 hours.

2. Spoon corn and beans into bowls. Serve with yogurt and black olives, if desired.

Makes 6 servings

Serving Suggestion: For a party, spoon this colorful vegetarian dish into hollowed-out bread bowls.

South-of-the-Border Macaroni & Cheese

5 cups cooked rotini pasta
2 cups (8 ounces) cubed American cheese
1 can (12 ounces) evaporated milk
1 cup (4 ounces) cubed sharp Cheddar cheese
1 can (4 ounces) diced green chilies, drained
2 teaspoons chili powder
2 medium tomatoes, seeded and chopped
5 green onions, sliced

1. Combine all ingredients, except tomatoes and onions in slow cooker; mix well. Cover; cook on HIGH 2 hours, stirring twice.

2. Stir in tomatoes and green onions; continue cooking until hot. *Makes 4 servings*

Simmered Red Beans & Rice

2 cans (15 ounces each) red beans, undrained
1 can (14½ ounces) diced tomatoes, undrained
½ cup chopped celery
½ cup chopped green bell pepper
½ cup chopped green onions with tops
2 cloves garlic, minced
1 to 2 teaspoon hot pepper sauce
1 teaspoon Worcestershire sauce
1 bay leaf
Hot cooked rice

1. Combine all ingredients except rice in slow cooker. Cover and cook on LOW 4 to 6 hours or on HIGH 2 to 3 hours. Remove and discard bay leaf.

2. Mash mixture slightly in slow cooker with potato masher until mixture thickens. Continue to cook on HIGH an additional 30 to 60 minutes. Serve over rice. *Makes 6 (1-cup) servings*

South-of-the-Border Macaroni & Cheese

Southwestern Stuffed Peppers

    4 green bell peppers
    1 can (16 ounces) black beans, rinsed and drained
    1 cup (4 ounces) shredded Monterey Jack cheese with jalapeño peppers
    ¾ cup medium salsa
    ½ cup frozen corn
    ½ cup chopped green onions with tops
    ⅓ cup uncooked long grain converted rice
    1 teaspoon chili powder
    ½ teaspoon ground cumin
      Sour cream (optional)

1. Cut thin slice off top of each bell pepper. Carefully remove seeds, leaving pepper whole.

2. Combine remaining ingredients except sour cream in medium bowl. Spoon filling evenly into each pepper. Place peppers in slow cooker. Cover; cook on LOW 4 to 6 hours. Serve with dollop of sour cream, if desired.   *Makes 4 servings*

Mexican-Style Rice and Cheese

    1 can (16 ounces) Mexican-style beans
    1 can (14½ ounces) diced tomatoes with jalapeños, undrained
    1½ cups uncooked long-grain converted rice
    1 large onion, finely chopped
    ½ package (4 ounces) cream cheese
    3 cloves garlic, minced
    2 cups (8 ounces) shredded Monterey Jack or Colby cheese, divided

1. Mix all ingredients thoroughly except 1 cup shredded cheese. Pour mixture into well-greased slow cooker. Cover; cook on LOW 6 to 9 hours.

2. Just before serving, sprinkle with remaining 1 cup shredded cheese.

                                                                Makes 6 to 8 servings

Vegetarian Sausage Rice

2 cups chopped green bell peppers
1 can (15½ ounces) dark kidney beans, rinsed and drained
1 can (14½ ounces) diced tomatoes with green bell peppers and onions, undrained
1 cup chopped onion
1 cup sliced celery
1 cup water, divided
¾ cup uncooked long grain rice
1¼ teaspoons salt
1 teaspoon hot pepper sauce
½ teaspoon dried thyme leaves
½ teaspoon red pepper flakes
3 bay leaves
1 package (8-ounces) vegetable protein breakfast patties, thawed
2 tablespoons extra virgin olive oil
½ cup chopped fresh parsley leaves
Additional hot pepper sauce (optional)

1. Combine bell peppers, beans, tomatoes with juice, onion, celery, ½ cup water, rice, salt, pepper sauce, thyme, pepper flakes and bay leaves in slow cooker. Cover; cook on LOW 4 to 5 hours.

2. Dice breakfast patties. Heat oil in large nonstick skillet over medium-high heat. Add patties; cook 2 minutes or until lightly browned, scraping bottom of skillet occasionally.

3. Place patties in slow cooker. *Do not stir.* Add remaining ½ cup water to skillet; bring to a boil over high heat 1 minute, scraping up bits on bottom of skillet. Add liquid and parsley to slow cooker; stir gently to blend. Serve immediately with additional hot pepper sauce, if desired.

Makes 8 cups

Broccoli & Cheese Strata

2 cups chopped broccoli florets
4 slices firm white bread, ½-inch thick
4 teaspoons butter
1½ cups (6 ounces) shredded Cheddar cheese
1½ cups low-fat (1%) milk
3 eggs
½ teaspoon salt
½ teaspoon hot pepper sauce
⅛ teaspoon black pepper

1. Cook broccoli in boiling water 10 minutes or until tender; drain.

2. Spread one side of each bread slice with 1 teaspoon butter. Arrange 2 slices bread, buttered sides up, in greased 1-quart casserole that will fit in slow cooker. Layer cheese, broccoli and remaining 2 bread slices, buttered sides down.

3. Beat milk, eggs, salt, pepper sauce and black pepper in medium bowl. Gradually pour over bread.

4. Place small wire rack in 5-quart slow cooker. Pour in 1 cup water. Place casserole on rack. Cover; cook on HIGH 3 hours.   *Makes 4 servings*

Vegetarian Chili

1 tablespoon vegetable oil
1 cup finely chopped onion
1 cup chopped red bell pepper
2 tablespoons minced jalapeño pepper*
1 clove garlic, minced
1 can (28 ounces) crushed tomatoes, undrained
1 can (14½ ounces) black beans, rinsed and drained
1 can (14 ounces) garbanzo beans, rinsed and drained
½ cup corn
¼ cup tomato paste
1 teaspoon sugar
1 teaspoon ground cumin
1 teaspoon dried basil leaves
1 teaspoon chili powder
¼ teaspoon black pepper
Sour cream and shredded Cheddar cheese (optional)

*Jalapeño peppers can sting and irritate the skin; wear rubber gloves when handling peppers and do not touch eyes. Wash hands after handling.

1. Heat oil in large nonstick skillet over medium-high heat until hot. Add onion, bell pepper, jalapeño pepper and garlic; cook and stir 5 minutes or until vegetables are tender.

2. Transfer vegetables to slow cooker. Add remaining ingredients except sour cream and cheese; mix well. Cover; cook on LOW 4 to 5 hours. Garnish with sour cream and cheese, if desired.

Makes 4 servings

Vegetarian Chili

Bean Ragoût
with Cilantro-Cornmeal Dumplings

Filling

    2 cans (14½ ounces each) diced tomatoes, undrained
    1 can (15½ ounces) pinto or kidney beans, rinsed and drained
    1 can (15½ ounces) black beans, rinsed and drained
  1½ cups chopped red bell pepper
    1 large onion, chopped
    2 small zucchini, sliced
    ½ cup chopped green bell pepper
    ½ cup chopped celery
    1 poblano chili pepper,* seeded and chopped
    2 cloves garlic, minced
    3 tablespoons chili powder
    2 teaspoons ground cumin
    1 teaspoon dried oregano leaves
    ¼ teaspoon salt
    ⅛ teaspoon black pepper

Topping

    ¼ cup all-purpose flour
    ¼ cup yellow cornmeal
    ½ teaspoon baking powder
    ¼ teaspoon salt
    1 tablespoon vegetable shortening
    2 tablespoons shredded Cheddar cheese
    2 teaspoons minced fresh cilantro
    ¼ cup milk

Bean Ragoût with Cilantro-Cornmeal Dumplings

Chili peppers can sting and irritate the skin; wear rubber gloves when handling peppers and do not touch eyes.

1. Combine tomatoes with juice, beans, red bell pepper, onion, zucchini, green bell pepper, celery, poblano pepper, garlic, chili powder, cumin, oregano, ¼ teaspoon salt and black pepper in slow cooker; mix well. Cover; cook on LOW 7 to 8 hours.

2. Prepare dumplings 1 hour before serving. Mix flour, cornmeal, baking powder and ¼ teaspoon salt in medium bowl. Cut in shortening with pastry blender or two knives until mixture resembles coarse crumbs. Stir in cheese and cilantro. Pour milk into flour mixture. Blend just until dry ingredients are moistened. Turn slow cooker to HIGH. Drop dumplings by level tablespoonfuls (larger dumplings will not cook properly) on top of ragoût. Cover; cook 1 hour or until toothpick inserted into dumpling comes out clean.   *Makes 6 servings*

Hearty Lentil Stew

1 cup dried lentils, rinsed and drained
1 package (16 ounces) frozen green beans
2 cups cauliflower florets
1 cup chopped onion
1 cup baby carrots, cut in half crosswise
3 cups fat-free reduced-sodium chicken broth
2 teaspoons ground cumin
¾ teaspoon ground ginger
1 can (15 ounces) chunky tomato sauce with garlic and herbs
½ cup dry-roasted peanuts

1. Place lentils in slow cooker. Top with green beans, cauliflower, onion and carrots. Combine broth, cumin and ginger in large bowl; mix well. Pour mixture over vegetables. Cover; cook on LOW 9 to 11 hours.

2. Stir in tomato sauce. Cover; cook on LOW 10 minutes. Ladle stew into bowls. Sprinkle peanuts evenly over each serving. *Makes 6 servings*

SLOW COOKING SECRET

Cut dense vegetables like potatoes and carrots into pieces no larger than 1 inch thick to make sure they cook through.

Hearty Lentil Stew

Vegetable Pasta Sauce

2 cans (14½ ounces each) diced tomatoes, undrained
1 can (14½ ounces) whole tomatoes, undrained
1½ cups sliced mushrooms
1 medium red bell pepper, diced
1 medium green bell pepper, diced
1 small yellow squash, cut into ¼-inch slices
1 small zucchini, cut into ¼-inch slices
1 can (6 ounces) tomato paste
4 green onions, sliced
2 tablespoons dried Italian seasoning
1 tablespoon chopped fresh parsley
3 cloves garlic, minced
1 teaspoon salt
1 teaspoon red pepper flakes (optional)
1 teaspoon black pepper
Hot cooked pasta
Parmesan cheese and fresh basil for garnish (optional)

1. Combine all ingredients except pasta and garnishes in slow cooker, stirring thoroughly to combine. Cover; cook on LOW 6 to 8 hours.

2. Serve over cooked pasta. Garnish with Parmesan cheese and fresh basil, if desired.

Makes 4 to 6 servings

Vegetable Pasta Sauce

Garden Potato Casserole

1¼ pounds baking potatoes, unpeeled and sliced
1 small green or red bell pepper, thinly sliced
¼ cup finely chopped yellow onion
2 tablespoons butter, cut into ⅛-inch pieces, divided
½ teaspoon salt
½ teaspoon dried thyme leaves
   Black pepper to taste
1 small yellow squash, thinly sliced
1 cup (4 ounces) shredded sharp Cheddar cheese

1. Place potatoes, bell pepper, onion, 1 tablespoon butter, salt, thyme and black pepper in slow cooker; mix well. Evenly layer squash over potato mixture; add remaining 1 tablespoon butter. Cover; cook on LOW 7 hours or on HIGH 4 hours.

2. Remove potato mixture to serving bowl. Sprinkle with cheese and let stand 2 to 3 minutes or until cheese melts.   *Makes 5 servings*

SLOW COOKING SECRET
Sprinkle a small amount of snipped fresh herbs over slow cooker dishes for a quick simple flavor enhancer.

Garden Potato Casserole

ACKNOWLEDGMENTS

The publisher would like to thank the companies and organizations listed
below for the use of their recipes and photographs in this publication.

A.1.® Steak Sauce

Barilla America, Inc.

Birds Eye®

Bob Evans®

ConAgra Foods®

Cucina Classica Italiana, Inc.

Del Monte Corporation

Delmarva Poultry Industry, Inc.

The Golden Grain Company®

Hebrew National®

Heinz North America

The Hidden Valley® Food Products Company

Holland House® is a registered trademark of
Mott's, Inc.

Hormel Foods, LLC

Kahlúa® Liqueur

Kraft Foods Holdings

Lawry's® Foods

McCormick®

McIlhenny Company (TABASCO® brand
Pepper Sauce)

National Pork Board

Ortega®

Newman's Own, Inc.®

Norseland, Inc. / Lucini Italia Co.

Perdue Farms Incorporated

Reckitt Benckiser Inc.

Riviana Foods Inc.

The J.M. Smucker Company

StarKist® Seafood Company

Tyson Foods, Inc.

Uncle Ben's Inc.

Unilever Bestfoods North America

USA Rice Federation

Veg-All®

Wisconsin Milk Marketing Board

INDEX